College For Every Student

College For Every Student shares best practices for raising college and career aspirations and increasing educational opportunities for underserved and diverse students in rural and urban districts. Providing guidance for educating your students and organizing communities for expanding educational opportunities, this is a must-read for every school leader and counselor interested in promoting educational uplift. This comprehensive guidebook offers a wealth of resources and tools for educators and professionals to help students build essential college and career readiness skills. *College For Every Student* gives you the research-based, proven strategies needed for promoting the core student skills essential for college and career readiness: aspiration, grit, perseverance, adaptability, leadership, and teamwork.

Rick Dalton is the Founder, and President and CEO of College For Every Student (CFES). Since 1991 CFES has helped more than 75,000 students in 40 states to graduate from high school and attend college. Dalton has written more than 130 articles and op-eds on educational issues.

Edward P. St. John is the Algo D. Henderson Professor of Higher Education at the University of Michigan, and serves as series co-editor for *Readings on Equal Education, Core Issues in Higher Education*, and *Engaged Research and Practice for Social Justice in Education*.

D0905764

Other Eye On Education Books
Available from Routledge
(www.routledge.com/eyeoneducation)

College For Every Student

A Practitioner's Guide to Building
College and Career Readiness

Rick Dalton and
Edward P. St. John

Routledge
Taylor & Francis Group

NEW YORK AND LONDON

First published 2017
by Routledge
711 Third Avenue, New York, NY 10017

and by Routledge
2 Park Square, Milton Park, Abingdon, Oxon, OX14 4RN

Routledge is an imprint of the Taylor & Francis Group, an informa business

© 2017 Taylor & Francis

The right of Rick Dalton and Edward P. St. John to be identified as authors of this work has been asserted by them in accordance with sections 77 and 78 of the Copyright, Designs and Patents Act 1988.

Library of Congress Cataloging in Publication Data
Names: Dalton, Rick, author. | St. John, Edward P., author.
Title: College for every student : a practitioner's guide to building
   college and career readiness / Rick Dalton, Edward P. St. John.
Description: New York, NY : Routledge, 2017. |
   Includes bibliographical references and index.
Identifiers: LCCN 2016009929| ISBN 9781138962378 (hardback) |
   ISBN 9781138962385 (pbk.) | ISBN 9781315659466 (ebook)
Subjects: LCSH: College preparation programs. |
   School-to-work transition.
Classification: LCC LB2351.D33 2017 | DDC 378.1/9—dc23
LC record available at https://lccn.loc.gov/2016009929

ISBN: 978-1-138-96237-8 (hbk)
ISBN: 978-1-138-96238-5 (pbk)
ISBN: 978-1-315-65946-6 (ebk)

Typeset in Optima
by Florence Production Ltd, Stoodleigh, Devon, UK

Contents

Figures

Tables

Boxes

Resources

Acknowledgments

This book benefited from support from colleagues at CFES and at the University of Michigan. At CFES, Kelly Larrow, Tara Smith, Kristina Hartzell, Karen Dalton, and Andrea McDonald provided technical support. Dr Ronan Smith and Dr Megan Kuster from TA21–CFES Ireland. Ken Aaron and Phyllis Stillman provided editorial support. Victoria Bigelow, Chris Nellum, Feven Girmay, Gilia Smith, and Brian Burt assisted with interview and survey. Several other practitioners participated in interviews, read sections, and provided comments. We sincerely appreciate this support.

Getting Started

A generation ago, a high school diploma was enough to ensure that students could get a good job and provide for themselves and their families.[1] No more! Today, a college degree is the new finish line. For most people, a bachelor's degree is the absolute minimum it takes to achieve economic well-being. And for low-income students, the best—perhaps only—chance they have to reach the middle class or beyond is by going to college.

But college access is declining, especially for low-income students. For millions of youth today, college can seem impossible to reach. In 2013:

- 45.5 percent of low-income students attended college, and
- 78.5 percent of high-income students attended college.[2]

That gap—we call it the "opportunity gap"—is higher than ever. It's growing, and it isn't likely to close any time soon.[3] Because while higher education has moved beyond the realm of nice-to-have and become need-to-have, teachers, administrators and counsellors in low-income schools are often overwhelmed and unable to provide students the support they need to become college graduates ready to enter the 21st-century workforce.

As the opportunity gap widens, the percentage of low-income youth enrolling in college this decade has declined. At the same time, corporate leaders have raised the concern that too many young people aren't career-ready when they graduate high school (Box 1.1).

The gap in college and career readiness for low-income students compared to their wealthier peers can't be solved by classroom reforms alone. College For Every Student (CFES) has pioneered practical strategies that empower low-income students to become college *and* career ready.

> ## Box 1.1 *The Skills Gap: Why Career Readiness?*
>
> Right now, millions of young people are struggling to find good jobs and launch successful careers, thousands of companies are unable to expand and innovate because they cannot fill critical positions, and entire regions hampered by slowing growth and stagnating living standards are looking for a cure. The common factor behind all of these challenges is a large and growing gap between the skills our children are acquiring and those needed for them to be successful in the 21st-century economy. It is perhaps the single most important factor limiting our aspirations as individuals, organizations, and regions.*
>
> * GE Foundation (2015).

We do this by helping students build college and career pathway knowledge and develop what we call the *Essential Skills* (grit, teamwork, leadership, and other competencies), tools that build social and academic dexterity, and open doors to a future that many low-income students may have never imagined possible.[4]

This guidebook provides resources that can help educators, volunteers, and outreach professionals build college and career readiness for low-income youth in urban and rural areas. You will be able to use the lessons and examples in this book to support middle and high school students on their own journeys to college—a process that the authors of this book have honed over the past four decades.

We began to work together in 2009, blending our work in advocacy and research. This book integrates lessons learned over our careers with a tried and tested approach that practitioners in schools, colleges, businesses, and community-based organizations can use as they help students find their own pathways to college and careers. You will learn about effective practices that form an evidence-based approach to building career and college skills.

The CFES Story

Three decades ago, *Frontiers of Possibility*[5] found that students who need the most support to prepare for college are the ones least likely to receive it. Since then, the situation has only worsened. As if teachers aren't burdened enough by increasingly onerous curriculum requirements, standards, and tests, they also have to help students navigate a litany of social ills, including substance abuse, domestic violence, and homelessness. As a result, teachers in many communities simply don't have the time to devote to college preparation and counselling, no matter how much of a difference those efforts can make to a student.

Expanding opportunities for students living in low-income communities is a critical challenge because:

- Increasingly, jobs that pay a living wage require a college degree.

- The number of students from low-income households is growing rapidly.

- Graduates with skills in science, technology, engineering and math (STEM) will have the greatest employment opportunities, but students from low-income areas are the least likely to pursue training in these fields.[6]

A critical component of aiding low-income students is deploying student advocates—volunteers from businesses, civic organizations, and colleges—as mentors and role models.

Why volunteers? One reason is that we believe all of us share an obligation to equip students to achieve educational and career success, especially when we have succeeded ourselves (Resource 1.1). More important, though, when low-income students look at peers and others from their neighborhoods who have gone on to achieve success, they find the encouragement to look inside themselves to take advantage of opportunities to move down the pathway to a college degree and, ultimately, a productive career that will lift them out of poverty. We provide a set of flexible strategies that practitioners can use that have worked time and again, in urban and rural areas.

Resource 1.1 *Tips for Practitioners on College Readiness*

How can you contribute?

Share your experiences. Offer students information and insights about college life that they may not find on a campus tour or college website. Be honest and open with students. Don't share anything you're uncomfortable with; filter any stories that aren't age-appropriate.

What should you let the students know about yourself?

- Tell students your name, age, and where you're from. Talk about your college, highlights of your experiences there, and your career goals.

- Describe how you felt about college growing up. Did you think of college as another crucial step in your education? Or did you only become aware of its importance after the fact?

- Talk about the anxieties you had about college before enrolling. Was it your first time living away from home? Did you think the work was going to be difficult?

- Tell them how it all turned out—how you coped with living away from home, how you managed the workload, and how college advisors and counselors helped you select a major and career path that was right for you.

- Feel free to ask *them* questions. Explore their interests and incorporate those interests into your conversations.

- Ask students to brainstorm a list of things to do to get ready for college.

Some examples are:
- study hard;
- visit campuses;
- talk to counselors and teachers about higher ed.;
- get involved in extracurricular activities such as sports, clubs, music, and community service;

- find out about taking the SAT or ACT;
- research colleges of interest; etc.

Strategies for helping students

- Tell them about campus life.
- Give them a sense of your pathway to college and the challenges you faced along the way.
- Get them to think about different types of colleges and universities, and how they can find a best fit.
- Help them understand the value of a college education.
- Help them explore financial aid and other options to pay for college.
- Generate excitement about the possibilities.

Origins of CFES

College For Every Student traces its roots to 1955, when Hurricane Diane—then the costliest storm in the nation's history—swept up the East Coast, killing and injuring hundreds. In Rick Dalton's hometown, Westfield, Massachusetts, a large population of low-income residents, mostly from Puerto Rico, were put out of their homes by surging floodwaters. At the time, Dalton was just a boy, but his great aunt, a teacher, brought him downtown so he could see the devastation firsthand. The memories that stand out—families living in tents in makeshift communities—had a powerful impact. His immediate urge was: *I want to do something to help.*

Eventually, those homes were rebuilt. Over the years, Dalton saw more intractable problems that couldn't be fixed by bricks and mortar. These issues stuck with him. At the Harvard Graduate School of Education, where Dalton completed his doctorate while on sabbatical from Middlebury College, he wrote about developing programs to encourage Latinos to become college ready. In 1986, Dalton went back to Middlebury and headed the college's efforts to increase the number of students of color.

During this time, Dalton joined a team of colleagues from the University of Vermont and Rensselaer Polytechnic Institute in a three-year research initiative, the National College Counseling Project, to study overcoming barriers to college access in disadvantaged communities. The project culminated in a lengthy study, *Frontiers of Possibility* (Holmes et al., 1986). Shortly after *Frontiers* was published in 1986, Dalton and another of the principal researchers, David Erdmann, who had moved from Rensselaer Polytechnic Institute to Rollins College, were asked to put their findings to the test in ten Southeastern schools. The results were dramatic: Over just a three-year period, the number of students going to college from those schools increased 50 percent.[7] Attendance went up, too, as did the percentage of students graduating from high school.

That success inspired Dalton to start an organization that would work with schools to help low-income children go to college. With a grant from the Clark Foundation, Dalton's group—then known as the Foundation for Excellent Schools (Box 1.2)–began its first project, working with eleven rural schools in and around Cooperstown, New York. Over the next fifteen years, Foundation for Excellent Schools worked in 300 schools across the United States, establishing programs to help more than 50,000 low-income students take steps toward college.

Three core practices (Box 1.3)—Mentoring, Leadership Through Service and Pathways—are at the core of the CFES experience. These practices help students develop the *Essential Skills* (aspirations, leadership, teamwork, grit, and other competencies) and build college and career knowledge (Figure 1.1). We wrote this book to encourage practitioners to use the core practices and the knowledge built by CFES over the last quarter century to help low-income students become college and career ready.

How CFES Works

Every CFES school has two things in common: A high percentage of low-income students and strong buy-in to the CFES process from school leaders. They also must have adequate resources to support the program, typically provided by a foundation, corporation, individual, or sometimes the school itself.

Schools select a portion of their student body to join the program. Most schools identify a minimum of 100 students; small schools, typically located

Box 1.2 *FES Becomes CFES*

In 2006, as part of a strategic planning process, Foundation for Excellent Schools (FES) leaders conducted 25 focus groups and 120 interviews with funders and school and college professionals to measure perceptions of the organization. Early in the process, it became clear that the name, Foundation for Excellent Schools, did not properly describe the organization's mission and focus. Although FES benefited students, it was primarily focused on school reform, a response to *Nation at Risk*.* As such, FES avoided some of the most-needy students because they often attended schools with high leadership turnover and chaotic environments, places where reform was highly unlikely to take hold.

During the interviews and focus groups, educators in FES schools were the only cohort that embraced the Foundation for Excellent Schools' moniker. They liked being called "excellent." But with more than 80 percent of the interviewees and focus group participants not liking the old name, "we needed to jump off the cliff. We needed to take the risk and change our name," said Rick Dalton.

Two members of the strategic planning task force, Binkley Shorts, a funder at Wellington Management who later joined the CFES board, and Karen Judge, head of development, came up with the new name, College For Every Student.

The old acronym (FES) was embedded in the new name, and most important, we accurately captured what we did and what we believed. The new name affirmed our commitment to putting students at the center of the process.

* United States Department of Education. National Commission on Excellence in Education (1983).

in rural communities, select at least 50; other schools select all of their students to participate. Then, before the school year begins, teams from each CFES school including students, parents, teachers, and administrators create yearlong plans at training workshops led by CFES staff. By the end of the year, every CFES Scholar is immersed in the three core practices.

Box 1.3 *CFES Core Practices: The Foundation*

Mentoring: Every CFES Scholar has a mentor—a community member, college student, and/or peer—who provides firsthand knowledge about the confidence, attitude and habits needed to succeed in college and beyond.

Leadership Through Service: CFES Scholars serve others, improve their communities, participate in ongoing leadership development, and create plans to share the benefits of their accomplishments.

Pathways to College and Career: To many students in low-income communities, college can feel like a foreign land. CFES Scholars visit campuses, meet college students and faculty, and get an insider's view of the admissions process, financial aid programs, and other aspects of college that can be hard for the uninitiated to grasp. Additionally, CFES Scholars get career guidance through mentors, role models, internships, job shadowing and other activities.

Each of these integrated practices helps students build the *Essential Skills,* contributing to their success in college and in the 21st-century workforce.

CFES Scholars and their schools have access to resources such as:

- *College partnerships:* Colleges and universities provide college students as mentors, host campus visits, and organize presentations to help Scholars and parents understand the financial aid and admissions processes.
- *Business partnerships*: Large corporations and small businesses provide mentors, internships, speakers, job shadowing, and other support to help students in their communities become college- and, ultimately, career-ready.
- The *CFES National Conference* brings together K-12 educators, college partners, business leaders, and students to network and engage in professional development and sharing of best practices.

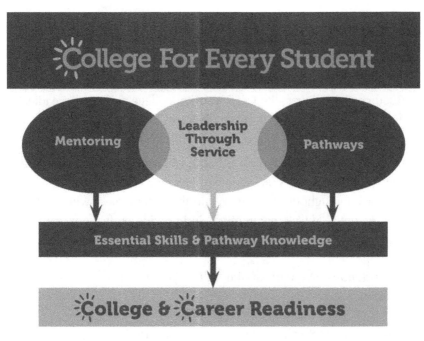

Figure 1.1 The CFES Framework

- *Peer mentoring, leadership development and college knowledge workshops* led by CFES professionals help Scholars develop the *Essential Skills*, improve study habits, and help students gain other competencies needed to succeed in college.
- Educators can build and strengthen relationships with colleges and universities through *College Connect Workshops* organized by CFES.
- Rising grade 11 and 12 Scholars can stay in a dorm, sit in on a college class and experience campus life by participating in *College Explore*, three-day programs at college campuses.
- *Professional development opportunities* take place throughout the year for educators to network and build programming that promotes college and 21st-century workforce readiness among Scholars. At CFES professional gatherings, educators share strategies they have implemented.
- Educators can confront new challenges and address existing ones at *summits* held at the CFES Center in Essex, New York. These two-day conferences focus on cutting-edge issues such as the skills gap, college

persistence, and corporate-education partnerships. While there, a small number of college presidents, school superintendents, and other leaders develop practical solutions captured in a white paper.

- *Virtual support* includes monthly webinars (CFES Live Chats), online resources and videos, the CFES website, college and career readiness apps, and access to social media platforms to share best practices and build support networks for educators and Scholars.

- CFES Scholars and schools are backed by *professional development services and resources* provided by CFES professionals, who visit each regularly throughout the year. While there, they meet with scholars, offer *Essential Skills* programming, and provide professional development for teachers and administrators.

Expectations: As part of the CFES global network, schools are expected to:

- Develop a CFES school- and community-based team composed of teachers, faculty and staff, students, parents, and community members.
- Appoint a CFES Liaison to serve as the point of contact with the CFES central office and the local CFES program director.
- Provide CFES professionals with access to CFES Scholars so they can conduct leadership workshops and peer mentor trainings, help develop Essential Skills, etc.
- Complete CFES Plan, Mid-Year and End-of-Year Assessments.
- Brand College For Every Student within the school and community.
- Track and evaluate program impact for the subset of CFES Scholars.
- Engage students in the three core practices: Mentoring, Leadership Through Service, and Pathways to College and Career.

School benefits: The organizing process, as explained and illustrated in the following chapters, supplements educational processes in schools. The historic and newly evolving models of public education are lodged in a theory that education promotes human capital. The old public school model moved this nation toward mass higher education.[8] The newer college preparatory model of high schools adopted by most states requires new forms of socialization, creating new barriers for students living in low-income communities (see Chapter 2).

Partner organizations: One of the strengths of the CFES model is that it is adaptable. This book will show how you can adapt this model to the needs of your school and replicate its success.

Several companies, educational institutions and other groups have worked with us to tailor solutions to address specific challenges they are confronting. Here are two examples:

Ernst & Young (EY) turned to CFES for help developing its College Mentoring for Access and Persistence (College MAP) program. College MAP is designed to help demystify the process of applying to and affording college, encouraging students who might not have considered applying for college to do so. EY professionals work with students to build the skills that will help them persist in completing their post-secondary goals:

- awareness of the lifelong benefits of earning a higher education,
- financial readiness that helps students apply for aid and pay for college, and
- persistence skills to help students complete college and succeed in careers.

Since launching in 2009, the program has helped more than 1,100 low-income high school students in 30 U.S. cities get on the college and career readiness path, with over 1,175 EY professionals having served as mentors. The program matches small groups of mentors with high school juniors, continuing with these students into their senior year of high school and throughout their college education. The team-mentoring model has several advantages: Multiple mentors provide insight and guidance to the students in the program; EY professionals are able to balance work and a long-term mentoring commitment; and the groups of students become their own supportive academic community.

Trinity College Dublin and CFES have collaborated through *Trinity Access Programmes (TAP)*, a partnership that employs the CFES model in 11 Irish schools. Several of those schools have gone on to become CFES Schools of Distinction.[9] Trinity College Dublin's partnership CFES is the basis for the "Irish Case" in Chapter 7.

Both of these CFES-adapted programs have many success stories. College MAP is the gold standard of corporate partnerships that other businesses can follow, while the Trinity College Dublin program has developed a strong research-based approach to building college access networks in Ireland. We hope that both of these examples, backed by quantifiable data, will inspire universities and corporations across the globe to collaborate with schools in low-income communities to use the socio-cultural support provided by the CFES framework.

CFES doesn't offer a one-size-fits-all solution; instead, each school uses the core practices to address the resources, culture, politics and other forces unique to them. The practical strategies developed by CFES and partner organizations can be used by other practitioners as they take steps to expand opportunity through empowering students.

Going to scale: CFES is committed to helping one million more low-income youth attain college degrees over the next decade. In order to make this goal a reality, we must enlist partners around the country to replicate the success of the Trinity College Dublin and EY programs. To make this happen, CFES will collaborate with colleges, businesses, communities, and other organizations. By embracing CFES' core strategies and processes and using the practical strategies listed throughout the book, schools and practitioners can employ the techniques we have honed over two decades. You might find our methods can solve the challenges that you encounter. Try these strategies and adapt them in ways that support students in your school and community.

Evidence-Based Approach

After an early career in policy research, over the past quarter century Professor Ed St. John has partnered with schools, colleges, state agencies, foundations, and nonprofit organizations to develop evidence-based interventions that promote social justice by expanding educational opportunities for students from groups underrepresented among college graduates.

Developing Evidence-Based Strategies

In the 1960s, St. John became painfully aware of social inequality in educational opportunity. When his Methodist minister returned to Napa, California, after participating in a civil rights march on Selma, Alabama, a cross was burned on the lawn of the rectory and he was soon run out of town.[10] The minister had previously supported integration in this white community. Since that time, St. John devoted his studies, activism, research, and teaching to promoting social justice.

Actionable research supporting social justice: After completing his doctoral degree at Harvard Graduate School of Education, St. John worked in state and federal policy, and as manager of policy studies in two private policy research firms. By 1980, national policy shifts had led to greater educational inequality for minorities. After the Reagan administration used his research on the impact of loans to rationalize increased use of college loans,[11] St. John decided to change careers. In 1989, St. John became a professor devoted to building practical knowledge about social justice in education. He has collaborated on research projects that informed development of:

- *Accelerated Schools:* A national network of more than 1,000 schools serving low-income students that employ organizational techniques and educational strategies to teach gifted and talented students.[12]

- *Indiana Early Literacy Grant Program:* A grant program for elementary schools engaged in improving literacy opportunities for low-achieving students in Indiana, which helped narrow the reading gap in the state.[13]

- *Gates Millennial Scholars:* A program that provided last-dollar grants to 20,000 high achieving, low-income students of color.[14]

- *Indiana's 21st-Century Scholars:* A program that provides academic and social support for low-income students who pledge to take steps to prepare for college.[15]

- *Indiana Project on Academic Success:* A statewide project in Indiana providing research and technical support for colleges developing retention strategies.[16]

- *Detroit Schools Higher Education Consortium:* A network of schools, colleges, and practitioners engaged in improving pathways to college.[17]

Learning from these experiences, St. John has developed an action inquiry model that practitioners and researchers can use to collaborate on evidence-based reform.[18] His recent books encourage researchers to engage in partnerships promoting social justice.[19]

In 2009, Dalton and St. John developed a partnership that has tied the continued development of CFES to data gleaned from current CFES projects and past research. Based on their collaboration, Dalton and St. John have co-developed the evidence-based method used in this book, an approach that practitioners can use to improve and expand educational opportunities for low-income students.

Learning to Empower Students

The evidence-based approach to organizational learning can help practitioners empower students from low-income communities in urban and rural areas, many of which have been hit hard by the displacement of jobs. Because of advancements in technology and globalization of labor, many good jobs once available to students who didn't go to college, such as manufacturing, have gone overseas.

We have found there can be a convergence of interests among educators, student advocates, and prospective employers in taking steps to ensure that students graduate with the skills essential for success in college *and* careers. The CFES partnership with St. John's research team has used an evidence-based approach for building the *Essential Skills* (Figure 1.2).

A learning model for college-access professionals: The CFES model builds *college and career readiness* (Figure 1.2, top left arrow). Using observation of and reflections on practice and informed by research, CFES has focused on building the *Essential Skills* for college and career readiness by adapting core practices and building networks (Figure 1.2, left circle). Organizing networks and engaging students in locally adapted core practices are the means CFES uses to empower students with the *Essential Skills*.

This research support has informed refinement of CFES core practices, especially the integration of career readiness and college affordability. St. John's team developed case studies of successful schools and analyzed surveys administered by CFES program directors (Figure 1.2, bottom arrow), which provide a basis for the evidence used in this book to depict how schools engage students in the core practices (Figure 1.2, right circle). The cases examined STEM-focused CFES practices, along with successful urban and rural schools.

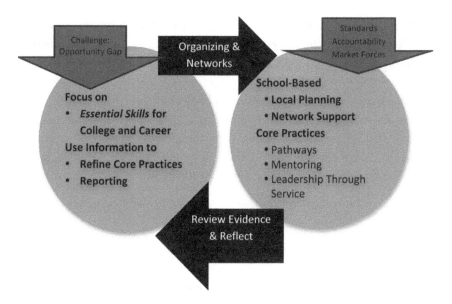

Figure 1.2 Evidence-Based Approach for Building Essential Skills for College and Career Readiness

The research revealed that required curricula, state standards, and testing actually *constrain* the capacity of educators in middle and high schools to integrate career content into their courses.[20] The CFES core practices help schools organize partnerships with colleges and community organizations that support socio-cultural development that empowers students to develop the *Essential Skills*.

Empowering students: We encourage practitioners to use evidence to organize student support in schools, including observations, reflections, and conversations with students and their families. We illustrate how practitioners can use quantitative analysis to understand how the core practices build *Essential Skills* among students. The core practices provide schools with a cohesive approach to student empowerment including:

- *Human capital formation*: Engagement in learning about college and career pathways empowers students to raise their expectations (*college and career pathways* practice).

- *Social capital formation:* Mentoring by supportive practitioners and peers helps students build the social capital for navigating education systems and career opportunities (*mentoring* practice).

● *Cultural capital formation:* Engaging in service projects and activities involves students in supporting the development of their own communities (*leadership through service* practice).

We refer to this integrated process of building capital for uplift as *academic capital formation (ACF).*[21] ACF provides a theoretical underpinning to the social transformations we see. The theory was tested by St. John's research on successful intervention programs that support expanded educational opportunities for low-income students and recent works by other scholars.

About the Book

This guide supports practitioners in their efforts to support low-income students get to and through college and ready to enter the 21st-century workforce by building pathway knowledge and developing the *Essential Skills.* When combined with coherent school planning for improved academic preparation, the core practices create opportunities for schools to transcend the constraints created by standards-driven accountability. The core practices provide a comprehensive approach to empowering academic capital formation by integrating socio-cultural support to strengthen the *education-as-human capital* strategy promoted by states and the federal government. In addition to narratives describing practical strategies, we use an evidence-based approach to illustrate how to build college and career readiness.

The practices are cohesive because they are developed through a school-based process supported by college-access practitioners in colleges and community organizations. The following chapters provide practical strategies and resources to help:

● educators to reflect on how their own practices empower students to prepare for college and career;

● college-access practitioners, volunteers, and community activists to empower students to build the *Essential Skills; and*

● college students and other mentors to develop mentoring relationships with middle and high school students.

Chapter 2, The Skills Gap: College and Career Readiness, examines the challenges facing low-income students in attaining college degrees and 21st-century jobs. In recent years, the gap has widened between available jobs and individuals prepared to fill those positions in the United States and across the globe. Readiness for those jobs and careers means attaining a college degree, and this requires that students, especially those from low-income households, receive help navigating their way to and through college. Financial hurdles, poor retention records at colleges, and other factors conspire to increase inequalities in college completion rates for low-income students. CFES offers strategies to help young people develop readiness for college and careers and ultimately narrow the skills gap.

Chapter 3, The Change Process: Organizing, Engagement, and Essential Skills, provides an evidence-based theory of change. Used throughout the book, college-access practitioners use this framework to:

● *build* community networks using the inner logic of academic capital formation inherent in the core practices;

● *engage* students in activities related to Pathways, Mentoring, and Leadership Through Service, and

● *reflect* on evidence from engaging in networks to inform improvements in professional practice.

Chapter 4, STEM Pathways, provides guidance that practitioners can use in moving middle and high school-aged students toward college and career readiness while focusing on STEM. The core practices empower students through engagement in STEM activities organized around Mentoring, Leadership Through Service, and Pathways to College and Career. Specific activities and tips focus on college partnerships, college exposure, STEM scholarships, STEM tutoring, mentoring, and internships.

Chapter 5, Urban Schools, discusses the challenges urban students face, and offers practical strategies to overcome hurdles, including partnerships with colleges, businesses and even other schools. The chapter also offers tactics such as adult- and peer-mentoring and student leadership development that build the *Essential Skills* and knowledge for college and career readiness.

Chapter 6, Rural Schools, focuses on the unique challenges facing students from rural communities. Many of the tactics to meet these challenges, including community scholarships and mentoring programs, leadership training, and high school-based college retention programs, transcend setting and are similar to strategies used in urban programs. The chapter also shares innovative examples of what rural practitioners have done to help their students gain college and career readiness.

In Chapter 7, Taking Action: The Irish Case, Cliona Hannon and Katriona O'Sullivan describe how Dublin's Trinity College Access Programmes is using CFES practices and theory to help thousands of low-income Irish students become college- and career-ready—and, in the process, transforming Irish schools.

Chapter 8, Creating New Futures, guides practitioners wanting to take more steps to help their students become college and career ready. In addition to summarizing and synthesizing earlier chapters, we focus on the tensions confronting schools, communities, and colleges, along with the prospects of building new approaches to empower students.

The Skills Gap

College and Career Readiness

According to some estimates, the United States will be unable to fill 23 million jobs over the next decade, while 20 million American youth, most from low-income backgrounds, will be out of work or underemployed.[1] The emerging strategy of developing thematic schools aligned with state standards has the potential to address these basic challenges.[2] In the urban market system, schools compete for external resources to provide socio-cultural support to help students build the skills needed to make informed choices about high schools, college majors and college financing.

The Skills Gap

In a perfect world, people looking for jobs would find available work. Unfortunately, it is more complicated than that. Employers frequently can't find enough appropriately trained individuals for currently available technical jobs, at least not at prevailing wages. Limited supply of qualified labor can mean that many jobs go unfilled. A growing number of corporate leaders and legislators call for solutions to close the skills gap, but this won't be easy because the gap is complex and immersed in both conflict and contradiction. Understanding the problem can help us begin to solve it.

In the United States, low-income youth are eight times more likely than their upper-income peers to be caught in the skills gap vortex, either un- or under-employed.[3] This is not because they lack ability or drive. Corporate leaders argue that skills training and postsecondary degrees are now necessary to claim anything above entry-level jobs. This rationale has been a major influence on the latest wave of school reform.[4]

In response, schools struggle to prepare low-income young people for the 21st-century workforce in the hopes of elevating them to the middle class, breaking a cycle of generational poverty and improving the competitiveness of the national economy. The challenge is to prepare as many students as possible to enter healthcare, technology, engineering, and other rapidly developing fields that now require a college degree.

Are You Ready? Do You Have a Plan?

College is a necessary step on many career paths, but many students wind up in degree programs without an understanding of why higher education is so important. We cannot expect students to put in the long hours necessary to obtain a college degree unless they have a real sense of what they stand to gain, and what it will take to achieve it.

For many students, getting to college is a huge accomplishment. But actually earning a college degree takes even more preparation and focus. Every student who aspires to graduate from college or attain a postsecondary certificate and find a well-paid job should develop a plan based on asking and answering the following questions.

- Why is it important for me to go to college and/or become certified in a skill or trade?
- When I graduate from college, what jobs will be in demand?
- Which of those jobs will pay more (and less)?
- What do I want to do in my career?
- What subjects do I need to study in middle school and high school to lay the appropriate academic foundation for the type of college degree or certification program that I want?
- How will I pay for college?
- Once I get to college, what challenges might I face?
- How can I cope with and overcome these obstacles?

We offer ways practitioners can help students develop their pathway plans and build their college and career pathway knowledge (Figure 2.1).

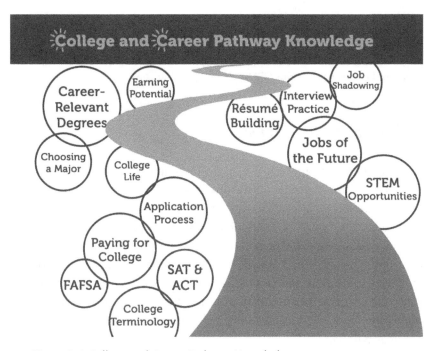

Figure 2.1 College and Career Pathway Knowledge

The Importance of a College Degree . . . Now More than Ever

By 2018, nearly two-thirds of the 47 million job openings in the United States will require some kind of post-secondary education. Projections indicate that three million of those jobs will be unfilled because not enough people will have the skills necessary to fill them.[5] At the same time, though, millions of people will toil in low-wage, low-skill jobs even though high-paying, high-skill jobs are available. The gap between supply and demand hurts people, companies, and entire economies.

While we can look to the end of the decade—and beyond—and know that the job market is changing, it is impossible to predict exactly what skills will be needed as it evolves. Technology drives change more quickly than we can develop programs to prepare students for those changes. That is why it is important for students to develop a range of skills and build an academic foundation that will not only prepare them for the rigors of college, but also leave them flexible enough to adapt to whatever careers they want to pursue in the years to come. "We must prepare students for a world that doesn't yet exist because 65 percent of today's students will be working in jobs that don't exist today," says Finnish educator and scholar Pasi Sahlberg, who spoke recently at the CFES "Skills Gap" Summit.[6]

College as an Investment

The evidence is clear: People who go to college earn more money over the course of their lifetimes than people who don't. And individuals who earn advanced degrees make even more, according to studies conducted by the College Board and other organizations (Figure 2.2).[7]

Of course, not every person who gets a doctorate makes more money than one who stops at a bachelor's degree. Earnings vary based on the quality of education one receives, the major one chooses, the technical skills one learns, and the job market. But the general pattern holds: *The higher the level of education students complete, the higher their lifetime earnings will be.*

If that doesn't strike you as very surprising, you might come from a background in which going to college is a given—an obvious step to take after high school. Students from underserved areas, though, don't always have college in their playbooks. And even though they would benefit

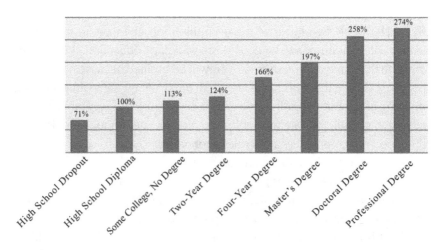

Figure 2.2 Average Lifetime Earnings of Education Levels in the United States Compared to Those of a High School Graduate

enormously from discovering the doors college can open, they are less likely to know just how important it is.

Career Readiness

Many low-income students lack insight into career opportunities. Students who don't know people who hold technical and professional jobs may not think it is possible to find one. It is crucial to provide exposure to these career pathways while students are taking required college preparatory courses in middle school and high school. It is increasingly necessary to have early exposure because students and their parents in urban schools are faced with choices about career pathways when they choose middle and high schools. The information gap problem must be solved to make progress on reducing the skills gap. That's a problem that can be fixed.

"There needs to be a clear connection between education and jobs of the future," says Kelli Wells, Executive Director of Education and Skills at the GE Foundation, which is working with CFES to better align college preparation with career readiness. "Educators, students and parents need to understand what kinds of jobs will exist so we can adequately prepare today's students for tomorrow's jobs."[8]

To make good choices, students need good information, such as:

- The jobs available today will likely be different than employment opportunities in ten years.
- "Middle skills" jobs (such as automotive and civil engineering technicians, and computer support specialists) are plentiful, pay well, and require two years or less of postsecondary education.
- Jobs in fields such as research science and engineering require a four-year degree, at minimum.

Employment possibilities must be considered by today's students. Educators should pair career knowledge with achievable, engaging and relevant career pathway lessons; without this connection, many students will have trouble making good long-term choices. We encourage educators to communicate with students during grades 6–9 so they can become aware of career choices and start down a corresponding academic path as soon as possible.

Adding Expected Lifetime Earnings to College and Career Readiness

Urban education markets with thematic high schools require that students make preliminary choices about their college majors while transitioning from middle to high school. When making these choices, students should also consider career pathways, because students from low- and middle-income families who attend college often accumulate high debt. Students should understand that expected lifetime earnings—and, perhaps, their ability to repay those loans—differ by college major type.

While it is true that many STEM (Science, Technology, Engineering, and Math) fields pay more than other fields, consideration of future earnings is not quite as simple as excelling in STEM courses. Preparation in advanced literacy—the symbols and linguistic methods in professional fields—is also necessary. While advanced literacy skills are secondary in math-intensive fields, most career specializations in science and engineering require understanding concepts—the advanced literacies integral to the field. Many careers in art and other fields emphasize interpretive skills—advanced specialized literacies—but they also require technology. Most career fields now integrate technology at higher levels than in the past: For example, graphic artists are more likely to work with computers than use drawing instruments, brushes, and paper.[9]

The evidence on earnings (Table 2.1), when broken down by the math and literacy intensity of required preparation,[10] reveals that:

- Careers requiring technical preparation include fields that emphasize both advanced math and advanced linguistic and interpretive skills. Understanding one's interests and talents is an important factor in choosing a high school, a college, and a college major.

- All types of four-year degrees have higher average lifetime earnings than high school completion, but students must weigh costs—including the hours they must work and the debt they can reasonably expect—against the potential earnings of careers associated with their major.

- Some associate degrees result in jobs that pay, on average, more than some jobs requiring bachelor's degrees. Given economic realities, students may want to consider a two-year degree in a technical field.

Table 2.1 Lifetime Earnings by Major for Interpretive, Critical, and Technical–Scientific Types (technical fields in *italics*)

Type (Preparation Emphasis)/ Expected Lifetime Earnings	Interpretive (Advanced Literacy Primary, Numeracy Secondary)	Critical (Requires Advanced Literacy and Numeracy)	Social (Requires Advanced Numeracy and Literacy)	Science & Engineering (Advanced Numeracy; Primary, Literacy Secondary)
College majors with lifetime earnings higher than the median for college graduates	*Architecture*	International Relations Political Science & Government	Operations/ Logistics Economics Business Economics	Engineering (most specializations) *Computer Science* *Construction Services* Physics Nursing Microbiology/ Genetics
College majors with lifetime earnings lower than the median for college graduates (but higher than the median for associate degrees)	History Philosophy & Religious Studies Liberal Arts Secondary Teacher Education *Film, Video & Photographic Arts* *Composition & Speech* *Music*	*Criminology & Criminal Justice* *Journalism* Communications Intercultural & International Studies Public Administration & Policy *Mass Media* Area, Ethnic & Civilization Studies Composition & Speech	*Human Resources/ Personnel Management* Geography Advertising & Public Relations Hospitality Management Social Science Teacher	Multidisciplinary Science Biology *Medical Technologies & Assistance* Environment & Natural Resources Health & Medical Administration *General Agriculture* *Animal Science* Math & Science Teacher
College majors with lifetime earnings lower than the median for associate degrees	*Drama & Theater* *Fine Arts*	Theology & Religious Vocations	*Social Work* *Family & Consumer Science* Elementary Education Early Childhood	

- Students with more literacy-intensive majors tend to earn less than half the average for all college graduates over their lifetimes. On the other hand, half of the math-intensive fields typically pay less over a lifetime than the median for all college graduates. In other words: Not all STEM fields are created equal with regard to earnings potential.

- Engineering has the most specializations with higher-than-average earnings. However, college graduates in more than half of the science specializations earn less than the median for college graduates.

- College majors in fields based in social (e.g., business and economics), critical (e.g., government and international relations), or interpretive (e.g., architecture) knowledge and skills have higher-than-average lifetime earnings.

- Some fields have higher earnings because a higher percentage of graduates go on to graduate and professional degrees.

Given the financial inequality in college access, along with the high debt facing most low- and middle-income students who obtain college degrees, students, educators, business leaders, and policy researchers must consider the net costs of college in relation to expected lifetime earnings. One of the reasons for this is the fact that the federal system of need analysis is woefully inadequate for students from low-income families.

The Gap Between Readiness and Opportunity

Educators can empower students to develop the *Essential Skills* by establishing partnerships with businesses, colleges, and organizations like CFES. Community engagement through service and internships helps students develop skills like teamwork and leadership. As we illustrate in this book, college student and adult mentors can help students build these vital skills.

Simply preparing students for college, though, isn't enough. An irony in the college access movement is that despite working hard to achieve college, growing numbers of low-income students wind up enrolling in less selective schools than they're capable of attending. Practitioners can help students build the skills to navigate the complex reality of college preparation, choice, and success.

Undermatching and College Choice

Even students who do everything right—take the correct classes, master important skills, and find their way to college—may not necessarily find the *right* college. Many well-qualified students, often from less affluent households, are not able to attend the quality colleges for which they are prepared. Estimates vary for the number of students who fall prey to this phenomenon, known as "undermatching", though the number in the United States is considerable. One estimate is that 28 percent of college students are undermatched, qualified to attend more rigorous institutions.[11]

More information can help students find a better college fit.[12] Even so, they must be able to pay the costs necessary to finish college and the long-term debt they may accrue during college: Long-term success is not just a matter of finding the right college, but also the right major. Unfortunately, students are often not guaranteed access to high-prestige and high-earning college majors. Students with merely average grades at the University of Michigan, for example, are often unable to major in some areas of business that lead to high earning positions.[13]

Students need to know how colleges operate. Mentoring programs that allow the exchange of realistic information between high school students and college students can be an excellent way to gain this type of essential, specialized knowledge.

Better-Prepared High School Graduates

In the 1990s and 2000s, reformers used successive waves of reports on high school preparation by the U.S. Department of Education[14] to advocate for higher graduation requirements. It worked: Most states adopted higher requirements.[15] But, as illustrated in Table 2.2, many low-income students graduate from high school prepared for college, but never go.

Preparing for college is no guarantee that a student will go to college. The American Council on Education recently reported that the overall college-going rate is declining for all students, in spite of gains in preparation, and the gap is widening for low-income students compared to students from high- and middle-income families.[16] Lack of information about choices and scholarships may be a factor; so, too, are basic financial

Table 2.2 Projected Rates of Bachelor's Degree Attainment of High School Graduates, by Family Income, Math Courses Taken, and Initial Enrollment (2012)

Academic Preparation		Initial Enrollment				Overall Bachelor's Degree Completion Rate	
		4-Year College		2-Year College			
1		2	3	4	5	6	7
Math Courses Taken in High School	% of Class	% Who Enrolled in 4-Year College	4-Year College Bachelor's Degree Completion Rate %	% Who Enrolled in 2-Year College	2-Year College Bachelor's Degree Completion Rate %	By Family Income and Academic Preparation %	By Family Income %
Less than Algebra II	34	8	33	34	7	5	22
At least Algebra II	66	40	62	31	20	31	
Less than Algebra II	25	16	38	34	12	10	36
At least Algebra II	75	53	67	28	34	45	
Less than Algebra II	16	23	53	39	29	24	55
At least Algebra II	84	66	78	22	44	61	
Less than Algebra II	10	33	65	46	33	37	70
At least Algebra II	90	78	84	15	53	73	

constraints. Many times, though, students have misperceptions about college costs that deter them from applying to elite colleges.

The cost of attending a private institution is often shocking. Even though few individuals ever pay the full sticker price—a fact lost on many students from low-income backgrounds—net costs are still high. Students who haven't watched family and friends navigate the college process may not realize there are numerous opportunities for financial aid. Unfortunately, they still must be prepared to borrow to attend most public and private four-year colleges.

Due to the cost of attending four-year colleges, college-bound students from low-income households often start in two-year colleges with the intention of graduating with an associate degree and continuing their studies at a four-year institution. Too frequently, though, they end up dropping out.[17] Two-year colleges allow students to continue to live and work in their home communities, as they are under pressure to contribute to their families while enrolled.

Many students who enter two-year colleges don't graduate. In 2009, only 33 percent of entering students graduated from two-year colleges on time. For African Americans and Latinos/as, the groups with the highest poverty rates, the numbers are even worse: only 24 percent graduated on time.[18] Starting at a two-year program not only slows the timeline to attaining a four-year degree, it also makes it less likely that any degree will be obtained at all. Attending a two-year college and continuing into a four-year institution may seem like a good choice, but students who choose this path should know the headwinds they may encounter.

Students wanting to attend for-profit technical colleges should heed the same warning. Like two-year colleges, these institutions have low completion rates: Only about 25 percent of students who enter for-profit colleges attain degrees. For-profit colleges also often have high costs that are less likely to be offset by grants and scholarships. Many students graduate from for-profit schools with weighty loans, a burden that can make it difficult to climb out of poverty. The problem is compounded by students who take out loans but fail to graduate—in those cases, they are left to repay the cost of an education that didn't yield a degree or give their careers the accompanying boost. Students who are interested in the trades need reliable information about costs, debt burdens, prospective earnings, and success rates before choosing their institution.

Low-income students encounter barriers to educational access and preparation practically from the moment they start elementary school. They can overcome some of these obstacles by learning about college and career pathways and building *Essential Skills* through engaging in activities provided through school-college-community partnerships that include local businesses.

Paying for College: Eyes Wide Open

Today, four-year and two-year colleges in the United States are more stratified by income than in 1980. College costs are much higher for today's students than for prior generations, at a time when degrees *and* career preparation are crucial for future economic well-being. Inequality in access has increased in recent decades.

A lost legacy: After World War II, the federal government viewed spending on education as an investment in both economic development and social uplift. In 1944, President Franklin D. Roosevelt signed the G.I. Bill, which allowed more than two million servicemen to attend college by underwriting tuition and expenses. The burgeoning numbers of college-educated veterans fueled the post-war economic boom.

The legacy of expanding opportunity continued to build over the next three decades. Created in 1965, the federal Educational Opportunity Grant Program provided funding for colleges to support low-income students pursuing undergraduate degrees. In 1973, Basic Educational Opportunity Grants (now called Pell Grants) were created, provided low-income students portable aid they could use at any college, further expanding access. These financial aid programs sustained the nations's trajectory toward equal opportunity. By the late 1970s, whites and minority students attended colleges at nearly equal rates:[19] But this period of equity was short.

The road to inequality: The Reagan administration reduced funding for Pell Grants, eliminated other grant programs, and required more students to take out loans, saving the federal government millions. (The shift to direct loans several years later meant the federal government actually profited from the loans.[20]) It didn't take long for the rate of middle- and high-income students attending four-year college to outpace that of low-income students. Low-income students were forced into low-cost, two-year colleges due to rising work-loan burdens at most four-year colleges. Only a few states have sustained funding for need-based grants at a level that ensures financial access and success to public four-year degrees without debt (Box 2.1).

The new federal policy framework, put in motion by *A Nation At Risk*, the 1983 report written by President Ronald Reagan's National Commission on Excellence in Education,[21] had improved college preparation for low-income students. Unfortunately, the growing number of college-prepared, low-income youth could not afford to attend the best public and private colleges because of high tuition, high loans, and excessive work necessary to pay unmet need.

The federal systems of needs analysis and funding for grant programs are inadequate for students from low-income families. Low-income students who want to step out of poverty must consider college costs and aid packages and choosing a major as part of realistic preparation for college. Some careers pay more than others, and accruing high debt may be a better decision for a would-be engineer than a would-be poet.

Restoring federal need-based aid to a level that ensures low-income students can pay for college would reduce unmet need: The net cost of attendance after grants and expected contributions. Accruing modest debt may be an appropriate way to cover students' expected contribution after their parents have paid what they can afford according to need analysis. Typically, students must borrow substantially more because loans have become part of the need-based award at most colleges.

Box 2.1 *A NYC Teacher's Message: Net Cost Limits Choices*

"I had kids with high-80 averages who were getting into selective schools like Syracuse, Wheaton, and American. They had an Expected Family Contribution of $0, but their financial aid packages still required them to cover $20,000–$25,000 of the cost—they just can't do it. As a result, they had to turn down their top choice in favor of a more affordable, but less desirable college." (Gregory Quinn, Collegiate Institute for Math and Science)

Mentors should help students understand the ins and outs of college finances, relating points such as:

- Students and their families are expected to pay a certain amount out-of-pocket to attend college, a figure known as the Expected Family Contribution (EFC). In addition, the federal government requires all students to shoulder a portion of their college costs beyond the EFC. Most public and private colleges expect students to use loans to cover the difference between their EFC and what they can afford to pay.

- Loans included in formal aid offers are not considered part of the Expected Family Contribution. Families without enough money to cover the EFC may need to take on additional work or debt.

- Many low-income families expect all family members to earn and contribute. As a result, many students borrow not only to pay their expected contributions, but also to help keep their families afloat economically.

Crossing the Finish Line: Degree Attainment

In the United States, the gap in high school completion is narrowing while the gap in college completion is expanding.[22]

- Only 22 percent of students from low-income families who enroll in four-year colleges actually graduate within six years compared to 70 percent of their high-income peers. If they eventually do graduate, most low-income students get a later start on career earnings and usually have higher debt.

- Almost half of all students who start college fail to complete a degree, leaving millions of working Americans without a credential that has become essential for economic security. While the United States used to lead the world in the percentage of the population with a college degree, it now lags behind more than a dozen other countries.[23]

Jeffrey Herbst, former President of Colgate University, described this as double indemnity: "Student loans are a reality today, so the real tragedy is when students face loan debt and they have no diploma to show for it."[24]

Learn about Student Aid and Hidden Debt

It is crucial that students understand costs when applying to college and can decipher what student aid offers mean when they are accepted.[25] Financial aid can be confusing even to families who have been through the process more than once. This FAFSA primer was created by a CFES school in upstate New York (Resource 2.1).

Resource 2.1 *FAFSA 101*

What is the FAFSA?
Free Application for Federal Student Aid.

How do I apply?
Submit your FAFSA form by the yearly deadline. There are three different ways to submit:

- Apply online at fafsa.ed.gov (recommended).
- Complete a PDF of the FAFSA to be mailed for processing.
- Request a paper FAFSA by calling the Federal Student Aid Information Center at 1-800-4-FED-AID or 1-319-337-5665.

What are the steps?

- Get a Personal Identification Number (PIN).
- You will need a Social Security Number.
- Gather information required to complete the FAFSA.
- Complete the FAFSA online application. Be sure to print and save a copy of the submission page containing your confirmation number.
- Follow-up: Check the status of your application a week after you have completed the FAFSA online.

What do I need to fill out the application?

- PIN number which you create at www.pin.ed.gov.
- Social Security Number.

- A copy of your parent's income tax return from the previous year.
- A copy of your income tax return from the previous year.

What are the different types of Financial Aid?
- Grants/scholarships: free money.
- Loans: money that must be paid back.
- Employment: opportunity to earn money for college expenses.

What happens if my parents are denied a PLUS loan?
If your parents are denied the loan, then you will be able to obtain additional unsubsidized Stafford loans in your name.

How long does it take to fill out the FAFSA?
The average time is 23 minutes.

A college's sticker price is just the starting point for a conversation about affordability. Here is a real-life example of how one first-year college student covered college costs with scholarships, grants, loans, and employment opportunities (Resource 2.2).

When students review the aid packages colleges offer they should consider:

- the hours they would have to work to earn their Work Study Program funding, based on their hourly pay rate;
- the prospect of unsubsidized borrowing if their families cannot afford their expected contributions (adding debt accrued from interest on unsubsidized loans); and
- the terms of repayment of subsidized and unsubsidized loans, including how much time they can stop to work without having to start making payments. Many low-income students find they must shift back and forth between periods of work and college in order to attain degrees.

Resources for Navigating College

Not all students who get a good start in college make it to graduation, but those who get a bad start are much more likely to depart before they finish.

Resource 2.2 *How One Student Financed Her First Year in College*

Total cost:	$21,120
(Tuition, room and board, books, fees, travel)	
EFC	$3,241
(Expected Family Contribution as determined by FAFSA)	
Financial need (cost minus EFC)	$17,879

How she pays:

Grants and scholarships:

Scholarship from college	$4,000
Scholarship from church	$1,500
State scholarship	$2,500
Federal Pell grant	$1,060
Federal SEOG grant	$300

Self-help:

Federally subsidized student loan	$3,500
Federal Perkins loan	$2,400
Federal Work Study	$1,600
Summer earnings	$1,019
Total	$17,879

It is important to have conversations with would-be college students not only about the challenges they will face, but also about the myriad resources they will have at their disposal to make scaling these walls easier. *Students—especially those who have had little exposure to college—often do not realize the extent of the student-support infrastructure they can use* (Resource 2.3).

Both four-year and two-year colleges offer students a wide array of services designed to cover basic necessities like housing, meals, and health, provide amenities like recreation, and identify career opportunities, internships, and job interviews. Though the names of the offices providing

Resource 2.3 *Common First Year Challenges*

Transitioning to college is a challenge for most students. Whether it's the first time they have been away from home or the first time they have had the freedom to choose what and when to eat or what academic/career path to take, challenges both large and small loom. The following are the most common challenges faced by first-year students.

Money, money, money
From understanding the different components of financial aid packages to managing "spending" money, students have difficulty making wise, sustainable financial decisions. They struggle to budget between wants and needs, and may find themselves unable to pay tuition and fees.

Making the grade
Many students struggle to adjust to academic life and are caught off- guard by the rigor of college courses. *Why?* Because they lack the Essential Skills and prerequisite knowledge to perform college-level coursework. Others get caught up in the abundance of extracurricular offerings and social activities that are characteristic of campus life.

Homesickness
Homesickness plagues most students at one time or another, but it is often most acute at the beginning and middle of a student's first semester. Being away from friends and family, and adjusting to an unfamiliar routine creates longing for the comfort and familiarity of home.

Time management and organization
Balancing class schedules and academic responsibilities with extracurricular and social activities requires a level of time management and organization that eludes many first-year students. Their grades may suffer, or they may be able to maintain grades but burn out in a futile attempt to take on too many things at once.

Professionalism

Whether rooted in the experiences of high school or time spent at a job, each student comes to a different understanding of how to operate as a professional. This manifests in a variety of ways that define (and, possibly, derail) a student during the first year: Interactions with peers, communications with professors and college staff, and attention to deadlines and details.

these services vary from campus to campus, they are available at almost every college and university (Resource 2.4).

One of the most important things students learn during college is how to build relationships with people who can affect their future. Students should use the strategies detailed in Resource 2.5 to open doors they did not know existed and build their networks.

Resource 2.4 *Campus Services*

Office of Business Services offers a wide selection of services ranging from books, food, convenience stores and cafés, on-campus printing and shipping services.

Dining Services manages meal plans for campus cafeterias and cafés.

Disability Services offers a wide variety of legally mandated services to students with documented disabilities, both physical and mental.

Financial Aid Office counsels students on financial aid packages and can assist by identifying potential additional sources of aid.

Health Services provides access to quality healthcare and encourages healthy lifestyles through health education, mentorship, and research. Go here when you need to see a nurse or doctor.

Housing offers information on housing in on-campus dormitories and off-campus apartments.

Libraries offer use of computers, printers, media, study rooms and additional research options. *Ask about discounts and classes on Microsoft Office and other computer programs, and additional media equipment such as cameras.*

Recreation Services manages gym memberships, fitness classes, and sign-up for intramural teams.

Career Services helps you meet career goals by providing services such as career decision-making, resume writing and critiquing, job interview preparation, job placement, and graduate school advisement. *Start meeting with these advisors freshman year!*

Student Organizations allow you to network with students who share similar interests and provide leadership opportunities. Most offer student development programs and recognition programs that enhance and introduce new skills. *Joining a student organization and being active is a great way to meet new people on campus, build lifetime relationships and develop a strong network.*

Resource 2.5 *Building Relationships*

1. Identify people who can have a positive impact on your future

- Make a list of possible future employers and identify specific people inside your school or community organizations who may be able to connect you to them.

- Create a list of key people at your college, such as the dean, dean's assistant, professors, and department advisors. Develop a plan to meet and network with them.

- Make a list of successful people in the career you are pursuing. Want to become a pediatrician or a lawyer? Find out who the top people in that field are. How could you get in contact with them? Follow their accomplishments, and note what was necessary for them to achieve their career objectives.

- Identify and join local professional chapters of associations relating to your field. This is great for networking and mentorship.

2. Utilize your network of mentors and professionals

Building relationships

- See your professors during their office hours, especially during the first few weeks of class. Most students will never use this opportunity so you will stand out. You will build a strong relationship with a mentor, and might even improve your grades by receiving one-on-one input about your work.

Maintaining relationships

- Stay in frequent contact with those you decide are good mentors.

- Remember to share both your achievements and your failures with mentors.

- *Do not* contact mentors only when you need help. Set up weekly meetings, or contact them on a regular basis regardless of your situation. Ask them about themselves too!

3. Utilize your network of friends and peers

Building relationships

- Identify places where people gather to talk about learning and spend time in those places. Introduce yourself to new people.

- Find nonprofits that you are passionate about. Most nonprofits have influential people as supporters who can interact with you in a non-professional setting.

- Introduce yourself to the successful students in your classes during the first weeks. Much of the learning in college happens by interacting with other students.

Maintaining relationships

- Do not reach out to friends/peers only when you need help.

- Most important in college, make sure your friends are having a positive influence on you. They will become your new family, and their decisions and actions will affect you.

4. Help people remember you by bringing something positive to the table

- Humor is a universal gift.
- Join discussions.
- Be engaged.
- First be interested, and then be interesting.
- Volunteer your time.

5. Commit to relationship building as a life-long discipline

- Start now! It's never too early—or too late.
- Think 5 years ahead in terms of relationships you will want to have, and make a plan NOW for how to develop them.
- Set aside time every day to reach out to people and make new connections.
- Create career-oriented social media accounts and use them for professional networking opportunities.

Providing Opportunities to Explore College and Career Pathways

In the older model of public education, students who prepared for and enrolled in college could explore different major and career options during their first two years of college.[26] As some secondary schools align their programs to career-related themes, many students are being forced to make these choices as early as middle school. One advantage of social support networks such as those provided by CFES is that students in thematic schools have opportunities to explore a range of college and career options and consider alternative pathways.

Build support communities: As long as low-income students are burdened with excessive loans, it will be difficult for them to work their way out of poverty.

- *Higher educational standards did not solve the inequality in enrollment.* Although substantial work is still necessary to improve high schools in urban and rural communities, there has been progress in educational preparation, but this has not decreased enrollment gaps.

- *A possible reconstruction:* America is engaged in a new period of high school reform that emphasizes alignment of career clusters and college preparatory content. The college preparatory curriculum constrains opportunities for teachers to integrate career content. School–college–community (SCC) networks can provide opportunities for more students to develop the knowledge and skills they will need to navigate college and careers (Chapter 3).

This modest reconstruction encourages students to consider careers that will make it possible for them to support their families. It falls far short of a solution to economic inequality, but it provides a strategy for contending with it.

Involve the community: The CFES core practices provide educators and community partners with a set of interrelated strategies to support students who need to make informed choices. It can be difficult for educators to support student engagement in local communities because required courses, aligned standards, and mandated tests constrain the time they have to address local issues. The accountability schemes used in many public school systems already place excessive demands on teachers' time. It is crucial that support networks add to the capacity of schools to meet students' learning needs without adding to the burdens of educators.

Leadership Through Service

Leadership Through Service is one of the three core practices of College For Every Student. CFES Scholars participate in this practice through leadership development and service activities. We believe that when young people serve their schools and communities, they lead, and when they provide positive leadership, they serve. Hence we see service and leadership as interrelated.

As part of service, CFES asks Scholars to help make their schools and communities better places and to take the lead in the design and implementation of service projects and activities. When students identify a need or problem within their schools or communities, they act: They have led projects including campus clean-ups, planned and led college awareness activities, provided math tutoring, and developed anti-bullying campaigns. Such projects make a real difference in a school and a local community, but they have a secondary purpose that is just as important. Students who build programs such as these from the ground up develop leadership, teamwork, adaptability, and other *Essential Skills*—the foundational skills they need to begin closing achievement gaps and focusing on college and career readiness.

College For Every Student has created an app called *Get Ready Now!* (Figure 2.3) that serves as a tool to help middle and high school students become college and career ready through interactive learning that scores responses to quiz questions about college and career pathways. *Get Ready Now!* has features that allow students to boost their college and career readiness score, track scores on a leader board, and tap into additional resources that will help them learn more about pathways.

Conclusions

Many corporate leaders and policy makers envision a future with more students prepared for careers that produce new technologies and an integration of technical skills into the new economy. Advocates of this scenario argue for improving STEM preparation in K-12 education.

It is crucial to recognize the urgency of this call for education improvement in schools servicing low-income communities. The chapters that follow offer many examples of strategies used by student advocates in schools, community organizations, and colleges as they responded to these challenges by developing networks with socio-cultural support.

Figure 2.3 CFES Phone App: Get Ready Now!

The Change Process

Organizing, Engagement, and Essential Skills

Box 3.1 *Shameka: The Role of Social Uplift*

Shameka had heard it before – and even began to believe it herself.

"I had been told that people like me never make it," said this graduate of Weill Cornell Medical College. "In my neighborhood, we never get as far as even finishing middle school."

Shameka grew up in Harlem, where she lived with her mother and her three siblings. As a freshman at Wadleigh Secondary School for the Performing & Visual Arts, Shameka was getting good grades and enjoying school. She was captain of the basketball team and part of the school's dance company.

"That's all I wanted for myself," she recalls.

The following year, Shameka's trajectory changed after her school began working with College For Every Student. "Once CFES came into my life, I never looked back," she says.

No one in Shameka's family had ever gone to college. Indeed, she is only the one besides her mom to complete high school. "CFES," she says, "transformed me as a student but, more importantly, as a person."

Before becoming a CFES Scholar, Shameka figured she'd get her high school diploma and then work at a fast food restaurant. That changed quickly. "After joining CFES, I became a college-bound student with hopes, dreams, and aspirations," she says.

As a CFES Scholar, Shameka became a leader at Wadleigh. "I learned some very important things from a CFES student leadership summit," she says. "I learned the importance of listening and putting other people first as key leadership ingredients."

Shameka not only shared what she learned but also inspired other students to take control of their own destinies and put college in their future. Shameka and seven other CFES Scholars formed a team called Da Committee to give structure and meaning to their mission, under the theme "Believing in Achieving."

Using the resources and opportunities available through CFES, Shameka and other members of Da Committee worked to get their peers on track toward college, serving as mentors and assisting peers in all aspects of the college application process.*

"Eight of us split the class, each helping a dozen peers find schools, fill out applications, and write personal statements," she says. "It was a long and hard task, but we were dedicated."

The result: Every CFES Scholar in 12th grade applied and was accepted to college. "One hundred percent college acceptance was amazing," Shameka says. "We showed the school that we could actually set a goal and complete it with little help from advisors. This may not sound like much to the average person, but to students in our neighborhood, it's like a fairy tale."

Under Shameka's leadership, Da Committee also planned and facilitated the first CFES New York City Student Leadership Summit, bringing together hundreds of their peers from Wadleigh and other CFES schools in Harlem, Brooklyn, and the Bronx.

The concept of students as leaders took off in CFES schools within and beyond New York City. The changes were palpable at Wadleigh, where Da Committee left an indelible mark.

Since leaving Wadleigh, Shameka graduated from St. John's University with a 3.9 GPA and completed Weill Cornell Medical College. Today, she's completing her medical residency in Los Angeles. "As a child, I could remember playing with a toy stethoscope but never imagined having a real one of my own," she says.

What advice would Shameka offer other CFES Scholars?

"Tell them this," she says. "Stand for what you believe, even if you have to stand alone."

* This effort, which began in 2006, became known as the 100 Percent Campaign. In 2016, members of the Classes of 2007 and 2008 returned to Wadleigh to help students in grades 11 and 12 become college ready.

Shameka's story illustrates how her engagement in CFES activities led to higher educational aspirations (Box 3.1). Her story is compelling, and it is a product of our strategy at College For Every Student—methods backed by an extensive body of theory and evidence. The 100 percent campaign spearheaded by Da Committee didn't just affect Shameka and her peers— many other families have been inspired by their message. This social transformation has had long-lasting ramifications: Many Wadleigh students attained college degrees and entered the workforce, passing their success on to future generations. Dozens of students from Shameka's class and the classes that followed are now contributing to their communities: Tony heads a nonprofit. Gregory teaches at a charter school in Harlem. Tiffany works in human resources at a corporation in Manhattan. Each of their stories affects and encourages others.

The CFES theory of change provides practitioners with a cohesive framework for integrating socio-cultural support into their schools. In this chapter, we discuss theories that are the scaffolding for our core practices. In the sections that follow, we focus on the three components of our framework:

- *organizing school–college–community networks* that support student socio-cultural development;
- *encouraging student engagement* in activities, which empowers them to take steps toward college and career readiness; and
- *building the Essential Skills* for college and career readiness through examination of evidence from successful programs, which provides educators with means of integrating social and cultural support into the curriculum.

Organizing Support Networks

The CFES organizing strategy involves local implementation of three core practices aligned with the socio-cultural development of college and career readiness. Shameka's narrative illustrates both cross-generation educational gains and entering into an elite profession—achieving *educational and social uplift*. Empowering students who live in poverty to pursue pathways that lead to cross-generation uplift for their families often requires access to knowledge about colleges and careers that is not readily available in their communities. That's one reason we rely so heavily on mentors: As individuals who have passed through social and cultural barriers, they serve as role models and provide trustworthy information. Students learn about their interests and career opportunities through service to their communities. Through their engagement, they overcome obstacles implicit in their social world.

Academic Capital Forms through Social Support

The theory of academic capital formation (ACF)[1]—family awareness of educational pathways and opportunities for pursuing them—reconceptualizes the uplift mechanisms related to human, social and academic capital formation that can be accelerated for low-income students when they engage in social support programs (see Figure 3.1).

Origins of ACF theory: Between 1997 and 2011, St. John and his graduate students studied three comprehensive college access programs that included guaranteed aid and socio-cultural support:

1. *Indiana's 21st-Century Scholars* provided social support and guaranteed grants sufficient to meet the financial need of participating low-income students.
2. *Washington State Achievers* supported innovation in schools serving low-income communities and provided guaranteed grant support for low-income students.
3. *Gates Millennial Scholars*, a scholarship program that provided financial and social support to 20 cohorts of high-achieving, low-income students of color, also provided leadership conferences and student support from national organizations.[2]

After St. John and colleagues developed ACF from their studies of these three comprehensive programs, subsequent researchers have further tested the theory. First, a group of leading and emerging scholars in the field of higher education collaborated on extending the basic ACF theory by examining a range of students by groups, including Latina/o, African American, and Hmong.[3] A subsequent quantitative study empirically validated the original constructs.[4]

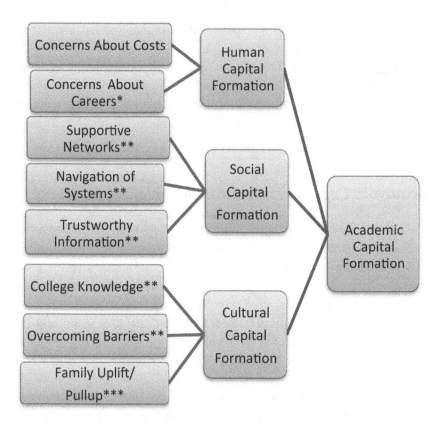

Figure 3.1 Research-Based Mechanisms for Academic Capital Formation.

* New construct emerged from research on thematic urban high schools. St. John, et al., 2015.

** Original construct validated in analyses of the independent survey and analysis. St. John, Hu, & Fisher, 2011, validated by Winkler & Sriram, 2015.

*** An original construct, separated into two factors (familial expectation and pull up) in the survey analysis. Winkler & Sriram, 2015.

Research on CFES refines ACF theory: Between 2009 and 2014, CFES partnered with St. John's research team at the University of Michigan to inform continuing development of CFES core practices. The research on CFES students helped further refine ACF theory. The insights gained from the research informed the ongoing development of the CFES core practices in the United States (Chapters 4–6) and Ireland (Chapter 7).

Through our research on CFES school–college–community networks and the students they serve, we have come to think of ACF as a *social transformation* process: Interventions that build academic capital increase the likelihood of localized social change along with cross-generation uplift of students and their families.

ACF uses a broader conception of the development of human capabilities than the older human capital paradigms. Instead of focusing only on financial return on public and individual investment, we also consider social and cultural capabilities. This overcomes barriers overlooked in the current reform frameworks (discussed in Chapter 2).

Human Capital Formation

Human capital theory, as introduced by Gary S. Becker in 1965, assumed students and governments made investment decisions based on costs and expected returns.[5] It provided a rational theory of investment decisions that was widely used in public finance and educational research. Human capital theory considered the market forces used in the education system in the mid-20th century, but opportunities to attend colleges increased as a result of federal student aid programs.

Becker updated the theory in 1975 to accommodate the development of federal student financial aid. Since market mechanisms have continued to evolve, it is essential to reframe the way capital formation works. Changes over the past three decades in America's educational market system require a further rethinking of human capital mechanisms. Reductions in the purchasing power of federal Pell grants after 1980, for example, resulted in an increase in the net costs of college for low-income students.

The development of college and career readiness as a goal for all students again changed the ways human capital formation works in American education. Social support that provides realistic college and career information is now crucial for college preparation, access, and success for students in low-income communities. More than one quarter of the CFES Scholars responding to our survey are in the federal free and reduced cost lunch program[6] even though they lived with family members who graduated from college.[7] These students realize they must acquire additional knowledge about college and careers, and build the skills needed to navigate the educational system toward career readiness.

Concerns about Costs: The decline in the purchasing power of Pell grants after 1980 corresponded with the growing gap in high school completion and enrollment in four-year colleges by low-income students. In the 1990s, researchers adapted education-attainment and human-capital statistical models to examine the impact of concerns about costs and confirmed its correlation with college enrollment.[8]

The growing gap in college enrollment for prepared low-income students compared to their higher income peers (Chapter 2) provides evidence that *concerns about costs* discourage low-income students from enrolling in college. After research proved that cost is a paramount concern among CFES students from rural and urban communities,[9] CFES began to focus on providing accurate information about college costs and student aid.

Concerns about Careers: The development of career education themes within American high schools forces many families with children in middle school to think about college majors when choosing a high school. Market-based high schools reconfigure the pathways through both K-12 and higher education.[10]

CFES has developed networking strategies and core practices to address career concerns within the rapidly shifting American educational system. This book communicates this adaptive process to the CFES community and to other groups willing to engage in developing transformative changes supporting low-income students and their families.

Social Capital Formation

After James Coleman's research found that whites left cities to avoid desegregation in the 1960s, he developed social capital theory in the 1980s to explain how groups maintain their social status: Students in wealthy neighborhoods had the networks, information, and examples to build knowledge for college and careers; students in poor neighborhoods did not.[11] In many cases, the movement to provide college preparation to students in all economic strata has neglected these three crucial sources of social support. Research on ACF used Coleman's three social functions as a conceptual starting point for identifying uplift mechanisms.[12]

Supportive Networks: In his original statement of social capital theory, Coleman argued that social networks function as forces that produce status through inherent connectivity. He argued that families could move, changing neighborhood, city, state or even country, to find networks that were more supportive of educational uplift.

The original ACF research found that supportive networks of peers, mentors, and counselors empowered students and their families to develop new patterns of connection promoting educational and career uplift. Through CFES, schools build these networks by working with colleges and community organizations to provide social support not available in low-income neighborhoods.

Trustworthy Information: As Coleman argued, "Information is important in providing a basis for action. But acquisition of information is costly."[13] Specifically, he said that the social environment in middle-class communities provided access to role models who encouraged education. Students in high poverty areas, on the other hand, had few role models, and lacked access to information for uplift. Studies of comprehensive interventions found that students acquired information about college through personal experience in supportive networks. Studies of CFES students and schools revealed that these crafted networks provided opportunities to gain trustworthy information through college visits, mentoring, and engagement in community service.

Navigational Skills: Coleman asserted that the social environment created bonds and obligations that could either support uplift or hold students in their communities. Acquiring the social skills to navigate education systems through trustworthy information is crucial to overcoming barriers in schools and communities.

CFES has developed *Essential Skills* that correlate to the skills college admissions offices frequently consider in their selection of students (Table 3.1). Required application essays give admissions officers visibility into the same noncognitive variables that William Sedlacek[14] related to students' capacity to navigate systems. The most commonly used methods focus on skills associated with college success.[15]

Cultural Capital Formation

Cultural Capital, first conceptualized by Pierre Bourdieu, has been used in studies of college preparation and choice.[16] Bourdieu used the concept to explain the role and value of education across generations of family life. He viewed cultural capital, in part, as knowledge of arts, professions, and

Table 3.1 Alignment of Noncognitive Variables, CFES Practices, and *Essential Skills*

Noncognitive Variable (Sedlacek)	CFES Practices and Essential Skills
Long-term goals Knowledge in a field Positive self-concept	Pathways to college & career (Grit) (Raised aspirations)
Realistic self-appraisal Navigating the system Community involvement Leadership experience	Leadership Through Service (Leadership) (Teamwork)
A strong support person	Mentoring • Adult • College student • Peer (Perseverance) (Adaptability)

social processes, and posited that cultural capital is to education what economic capital is to money.[17] ACF research has focused on three mechanisms (college knowledge, cross-generation communication about education, and school–college–community networks) that provide the cultural support necessary to lift students and their families.[18]

College Knowledge: Bourdieu's theory argues that differences in cultural capital explain educational and class differences: Schools serving low-income students transmit different forms of class-related cultural capital than schools serving the economic elite among whom college is expected. In her groundbreaking 1997 book, *Choosing Colleges: How Social Class and Schools Structure Opportunity,* Patricia M. McDonough demonstrates that even in schools in wealthy suburbs, low-income students receive different counseling and college information than their wealthier peers.[19] Her book stimulated subsequent research on college knowledge.

The original ACF studies found that social support networks helped students build knowledge to navigate educational systems.[20] Indiana's 21st-century Scholars benefited from mentors, while their parents benefited from college visits and other support. Washington State Achievers attributed insights about college options to guidance they received from mentors. Gates Millennial Scholars benefited from information on graduate programs in

STEM education and public health provided through leadership courses and networks; they attended graduate school at much higher rates than comparable peers. (In all three of these programs, however, supplemental financial incentives proved to be as important as information provided by networks.)

As social and economic standards shift, the developing expectation that all students should prepare for college radically alters the necessity for college and career knowledge. Understanding college and career pathways is now a form of cultural capital all students need. The research on CFES students reported in *Left Behind: Urban High Schools and the Failure of Market Reform*[21] shows how college and career knowledge delivered via school–college–community (SCC) networks and embedded CFES core practices empowers low-income students.

Overcoming barriers refers specifically to using trustworthy information and social support through networks to transcend educational barriers. Overcoming social and financial barriers is at the core of transforming social reproduction into cross-generation uplift.

CFES is a powerful force for supporting cultural capital formation by students who live in high poverty areas.[22] They learn from mentors, visiting colleges, and planning and organizing events in their communities. Through these experiences, students build skills that help them overcome financial, educational, and social barriers that are embedded in low-income communities and their schools.

Cross-generation communication about education: One of Bourdieu's foundational arguments has been that *habitus*,[23] or habitual patterns reinforced in families and communities, reproduce social class. Social attainment research consistently finds that students are likely to go into occupations similar to their parents. While schools now routinely send formal messages about college and more students are academically prepared for college upon graduating from high school, improvements in college access have lagged. Analyses of interviews with students in all four large-scale interventions (Washington State Achievers (WSA), Gates Millennial Scholars (GMS), Twenty-first Century Scholars (TFCS), and CFES) indicate that communication and changing expectations within students' families is vital to increase the likelihood of college going.

In the 20th-century education system, most students completed one of three high school tracks: Advanced college preparation for high-achieving students; general education for the majority of students who might go to college or directly to work; and vocational preparation. Requiring all schools to provide college-preparatory instruction beginning in the early 2000s essentially eliminated the general diploma and limited the capacity of schools to provide vocational training due to curricular constraints. School–college–community networks provide social support through mentoring and career and college pathways knowledge. When students join CFES, they commit to learn about college and career, work closely with mentors and become mentors to younger students, develop leadership competencies, and participate in service activities.

School–college–community networks: Too often, high schools in low-income communities and colleges don't work together. In her review of the research on ACF, Rachelle Winkle-Wagner noted how organizing strategies between fields can foster college readiness:

> If we consider ways one field (social context) might be bridged to another, we might be better able to holistically consider improved access to college for underrepresented students. The empirical studies in this volume suggest exactly this even without explicitly saying so: many of the chapters presented evidence of ways families, communities, schools, and higher education institutions were connected in the lives of prospective college students. These are connections between *fields* that might allow for the kind of social transformation that those of us who study issues of educational equity want to foster.[24]

Winkle-Wagner's framework illustrates how SCC networks can promote educational uplift through Academic Capital Formation (ACF) (Figure 3.2). Networks supporting ACF function at the intersection of schools, colleges, and communities.

A transformation is underway in American education. Building networks that provide social support for students in low-income communities is a crucial step forward.

Student Engagement in Core Practices

School–college–community networks provide socio-cultural support and engage students in empowering practices that build college and career

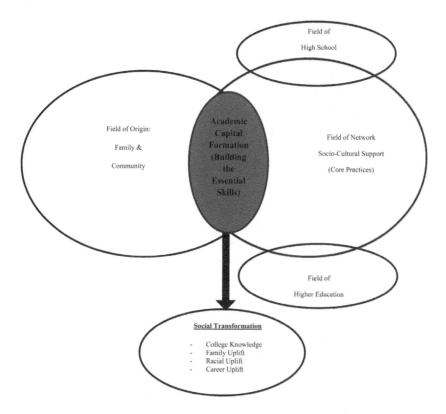

Figure 3.2 Academic Capital Formation and Essential Skills: Connecting
Fields of Origin and School–College–Community Networks
Supporting College Preparation. Adapted from Winkle-
Wagner (2012).

readiness. Students must choose to participate in the activities offered. The CFES model recognizes the importance of inviting students to engage, rather than requiring their participation.

Activities related to core practices are organized within each school–college network. Students provide input into the local activities, often helping organize them through voluntary service. While student engagement is voluntary, it is also vital to the development of the knowledge and skills for navigating college and career pathways. Each network develops strategies for encouraging student engagement. For example, the CFES Pledge developed at a K-6 school in Hawaii helps its students understand and commit to the values of College For Every Student.

CFES Pledge—August Ahrens Elementary School (AAES)

I will **ASPIRE** to go to college
I will **ADAPT** to any situation and be a problem solver
I will **EXCEL** and try my best in everything I do
I will **SERVE** my home, school, and community and be a leader
College For Every Student, College For Me!

Comparing a survey of CFES Scholars (N=940) to one with students at Slade Middle School (N=103), a non-CFES school whose students are from a similar socioeconomic status background, provides strong evidence that participation in the pathways practice builds knowledge about college attendance and admission.

The majority of the comparison group from Slade was in 8th grade, with 45 percent in the 6th and 7th grades (Table 3.2). In contrast, the CFES Scholars were more evenly distributed across grades 6 through 8, though a few students were in 9th and 10th grades. More than 60 percent of respondents in both groups were in the federal free and reduced-cost lunch program, indicating they met federal criteria for poverty, although a higher percentage of students in Slade did not know whether they were in the federal program. (It should be noted that middle and high school students and their families often under-report levels of poverty.)

There were differences in the racial/ethnic composition of the two groups. A higher percentage of Slade's students were Latino and African American, while higher percentages of CFES Scholars were Caucasian and Asian. Slade's racial/ethnic composition was more similar to urban (Chapter 5) than rural (Chapter 6) CFES Scholars.

Engagement in College and Career Pathways

There were many striking differences between the CFES Scholars and their counterparts in the non-CFES school (Table 3.3), including:

- Only 20 percent of the students from Slade indicated they knew about financial aid compared to 91 percent of the CFES Scholars.
- No Slade students indicated a college representative had visited their school, compared to 55 percent of CFES Scholars.

Table 3.2 Comparison of CFES Scholars and Control Group

A. Grade Levels		
	Slade %	CFES %
6th grade	20	22
7th grade	25	26
8th grade	53	31
9th grade	1	12
10th grade	0	8
Total	100	100
B. Self-Reported Participation in Federal Free and Reduced Cost Lunch		
	Slade %	CFES %
Yes	65	64
No	11	25
Don't know	24	11
No response	0	0
C. Race/Ethnicity of Respondents		
	Slade %	CFES %
Caucasian or White, not Hispanic	12	40
Black or African American	29	21
American Indian or Alaska Native	NA	1
Latino/a or Hispanic	38	14
Asian, Native Hawaiian or Other Pacific Islander	6	18
No response	15	5

- Almost all CFES Scholars—92 percent—thought they would need to improve their grades to get into the best colleges, while only about half of Slade students thought this to be true.

The surveys also show that student engagement in college networks helps raise aspirations (Table 3.4). While 65 percent of CFES Scholars

Table 3.3 Engagement in College/Career Pathways Practices by Scholars and
Control Group

	Slade %	CFES %
CFES scholar (self-identify)	0	93
Talked to college student last year	3	71
College students visited my school last year	4	63
College representative visited last year	0	55
Visited college campus last year	19	79
I know about financial aid/scholarships	20	91
I know the courses I need for college	27	72
I talk with my family about college	Not asked	81
Need to improve grades for best college	50	92

planned to attend a four-year college, 43 percent of Slade students did not know what they would be doing after high school and just 37 percent were expecting to go to a four-year college.

Engagement in Mentoring and Social Support

Mentoring is one of the pillars of the CFES program, so it is not surprising that most CFES Scholars report having an adult mentor. That stands in stark contrast to Slade, where just 15 percent of students have a mentor (Table 3.5). Most CFES Scholars indicated their mentors not only made it easy to ask questions, but also encouraged them to think about college. Mentors at CFES institutions include peers, adults, and college students. Educators in schools frequently take on informal roles as mentors as part of their work as teachers, counselors, and staff, while peer mentoring builds a culture of respect and care in schools.

At CFES schools, mentoring is self-perpetuating: Just as students are expected to work with mentors, they are expected to become mentors themselves at some point (Box 3.2). Indeed, almost half of CFES students say they act as mentors, compared to fewer than one in ten at Slade.

Table 3.4 Plans for the Year After High School: CFES Scholars and Control Group

	Slade %	CFES %
Work	7	6
Go to a trade or technical school	7	2
Attend a two-year or community college	7	7
Attend a four-year college or university	37	65
Don't know	43	11
No response	5	10

Table 3.5 Engagement in Mentoring and Social Support: CFES Scholars and Control Group

	Slade %	CFES %
I know college dropouts	N/A	51
Talked with older student about problems	N/A	38
Older student is a mentor	12	42
Adult mentor (teacher, counselor, other)	15	63
Mentor makes it easy to ask questions	N/A	72
Teachers encourage college plans	46	88
Mentor encourages me to think about college	13	74
I am a mentor	7	45

Engagement in Leadership Through Service

Leadership Through Service provides opportunities for students to contribute to the civic good while exploring possible career pathways. CFES Scholars build their leadership skills by planning service projects and leading workshops, mentoring, and other activities. While student government traditionally provides these opportunities to small groups of students in middle and high school, the CFES Leadership Through Service practice extends these opportunities to all Scholars (Box 3.3).

Box 3.2 *Peer Mentoring*

Kennedy is a sixth grader at New York's Edmeston Central School; Alexis, a senior at Edmeston Central, is her mentor. Their relationship, though, is hardly a one-way street. Both students gain from the relationship—a phenomenon that we see again and again at CFES.

The girls quickly discovered they have much in common. Both take part in activities outside of school—Kennedy is a horseback rider, Alexis a dancer. These activities provide a second social circle apart from school friends.

Alexis helped Kennedy understand that engaging with a separate group of friends through horseback riding, dancing, or some other activity can create a place to feel welcome and supported. "It's nice to know that someone older cares and has gone through similar experiences," Kennedy said of her mentor.

But Alexis has also benefited from the relationship. "I enjoy mentoring," she said. "It's opened my eyes to what younger kids are dealing with today."

Through mentoring, students like Alexis and Kennedy develop the *Essential Skills*—teamwork, adaptability, grit, leadership, and other competencies—that not only help them deal with problems today, but build the skills necessary to succeed in college and the workplace.

"Our CFES mentoring program is informal by design," said Edmeston guidance counselor Katie Russell. "Our students don't see mentoring as an assignment. Parents or teachers refer elementary kids who would benefit from mentoring, and we pair them with a suitable mentor from a pool of high school students."

While mentors and mentees are developing the *Essential Skills*, they are also having fun. According to Russell, enjoyment of mentoring is contagious. "As the year progresses, more and more high school students sign up to be mentors when they hear about it from their friends," she said. "Personally, working on mentoring is my favorite part of the job—I wish I could do this all day long."

Box 3.3 *Leadership Through Service Builds Career Knowledge*

Students at Booker Middle School in Florida are years from reaching the workforce. In designing a Dress For Success workshop with a local job placement center, though, they not only helped job seekers in their community, but also learned critical career insights that will serve them in the future. By developing interview tips for job seekers, helping job seekers find appropriate workplace clothing and even assembling a job fair, the Booker students had a lasting impact on their community.

Working with CFES Scholars and the Fashion Club at Booker High, the middle school students launched a clothing drive to collect new and gently worn business attire. After steaming the clothes and carefully displaying them in a space they called the Brighter Futures Boutique, the students opened the doors to job seekers in desperate need of appropriate job-hunting attire. Not everybody's wardrobe includes shirts, ties or dresses—and the boutique offered an upscale, respectful way of offering these items.

Over 30 companies sent a total of 100 representatives to the job fair, which was attended by 150 people. "We were able to witness people line up job interviews for the next week," said Booker Middle School principal LaShawn Frost.

It was a complete success. The principal was so elated that she immediately started planning for next year. CFES helped the school form invaluable partnerships through this endeavor. Everyone was impressed by the fact that the students were the driving force, and they were very humbled to be a part of it. The remaining career wear that was collected for the clothing drive was donated to the Career Source Closet, a professionally run version of the students' boutique.

By engaging in Leadership Through Service activities, students see themselves as leaders (Table 3.6). More CFES Scholars were engaged in service activities, collaborated with other students on out-of-class projects, and worked with other students to solve problems than their non-CFES counterparts; they also indicated that other students sought their opinions. This type of engagement helps students build leadership and teamwork skills.

Table 3.6 Engagement in Leadership Through Service: CFES Scholars and Control Group

	Slade %	CFES %
Involved in service activities	4	47
Students seek my opinion	N/A	78
See self as a leader	59	80
Community service through school	N/A	76
Worked with other students on out-of-class Projects	42	62
Worked with other students to solve problems	43	68
Served as a mentor or coach to younger students	16	40
Organized activities for student groups	14	30
Learned about project planning and team work	47	59

Building Essential Skills

Educators are inundated by curricular mandates to support a growing body of educational and accountability standards. In addition, professional associations in teacher education, math education, counseling, and other specializations promote their own lists of skills to impart, some of which are included in state standards. The *Essential Skills* developed by CFES provide support for educators and build strong school cultures.

The National Research Council's study, *Education and Work Life: Developing Transferable Knowledge and Skills for the 21st Century*, advocates developing measurable indicators to be used for assessment as part of public accountability,[25] and most states include skills development as part of educational standards. Unfortunately, this approach of standardizing skill sets often constrains the capacity of educators to support sociocultural skill development.[26]

A Practical Approach to Essential Skills

The core practices CFES champions may have at one time been considered ancillary to a thorough K-12 education. Increasingly, they must be integral because the social aspects of college and career readiness are critical to student success. While the CFES *Essential Skills* provide a straightforward approach, we also recognize that educators and college-access professionals may have to contend with skill requirements related to state standards and specialized content.

Achieve, Inc., [27] one of the many advocacy organizations engaged in promoting standards-based reform, has developed a comprehensive set of skills we use here for illustrative purposes, many of which overlap with CFES *Essential Skills* (Table 3.7). Since Achieve, Inc.'s list includes many skills emphasized in the Common Core State Standards (CCSS), practitioners in some schools may find these skills are part of the accountability frameworks used in their states.

Specialized content skills: In addition to the lists of skills advocated by states using standards-driven rubrics, professional associations of educators also recommend skill sets aligned with the priorities of those individual fields. With the development of career themes, career-oriented college-prep high schools, STEM-pathways strategies, and other academic interventions in schools, educators are confronted by specialized skills lists as part of their work.

For example, the Career and Technical Education (CTE) skill set focuses explicitly on formation of human capital, and treats social and cultural development as secondary to academic content (Box 3.4). The social support provided by school-college networks can actually help with the development of these skills.

CFES Essential Skills: The CFES *Essential Skills* for college and career readiness were developed by CFES over the last 20-plus years working with schools, community-based organizations, corporations and foundations, program professionals, and students (Box 3.5). The definitions used in the

Table 3.7 Alignment of CFES Core Practices to Achieve, Inc.'s List of CCSS and non-CCSS Essential Skills

CFES Practices	Essential Skills in CCSS	Essential Skills Not in CCSS
Pathways to College and Career	Use of data (for college and/or career choice) Use of research skills (for college and/or career choice)	Job-seeking skills Career planning and exploration Workplace health and safety
Leadership Through Service	Teamwork/collaboration skills Problem-solving skills Application/extension of content in various situations Time-management skills Use of technology (in ELA/literacy)	Recognizing personal strengths and weaknesses Ethical reasoning Conflict resolution skills Technology-based project-management skills Quality control and system practices
Mentoring Adult–Student Peer	Communication skills Reasoning skills	External and internal work-based communication skills Motivation/discipline skills Adaptability skills

Box 3.4 *Career and Technical Education (CTE) Essential Skills Advocated by the National Association of State Directors of Career and Technical Education Consortium**

1. *Academic foundations:* Achieve additional academic background and skills required to pursue a full range of career and post-secondary education opportunities within a career cluster.

2. *Problem solving and critical thinking:* Solve problems using critical thinking skills independently and in teams. Solve problems using creativity and innovation.

3. *Information technology applications:* Use information technology tools specific to the cluster to access, manage, and integrate and create information.

4. *Systems:* Understand role within teams, work units, departments, organizations, inter-organizational systems and the larger environment. Identify how key organization systems affect performances and the quality of products and services. Understand global context of industries and careers.

5. *Safety, health and environment:* Understand the importance of health, safety, and environmental management systems in organizations, and their importance to organizations, organizational performance and regulatory compliance.

6. *Leadership and teamwork:* Use leadership and teamwork skills while collaborating with others to accomplish organizational goals and objectives.

7. *Ethics and legal responsibilities:* Know and understand the importance of professional ethics and legal responsibilities.

8. *Employment and career development:* Know and understand the importance of employability skills. Explore, plan and effectively manage careers. Know and understand the importance of entrepreneurship skills.

9. *Technical skills:* Use technical knowledge and skills required to pursue careers in all career clusters, including knowledge of design, operation and maintenance of technological systems critical to the career cluster.

* Achieve (2012, p. 5).

CFES *Essential Skills* are aligned with the research literature. They are also consonant with our working theory of social transformation. Chapter 5 shows how urban programs support students, while Chapter 6 illustrates the development of the same skill set among rural students.

Box 3.5 *CFES Essential Skills for College and Career Readiness*

1. *Grit*: Determination and passion for long-term goals.*

2. *Leadership:* Problem solving through problem- and project-based learning.**

3. *Teamwork:* Collaboration on projects involving communication and problem solving.***

4. *Raised aspirations:* Overcome barriers to setting higher education goals.****

5. *Perseverance*: Toughness and internal strength that helps individuals achieve long term goals.*****

6. *Adaptability*: Flexibility when working with people with different views and cultures.******

* Duckworth, Peterson, Matthews, & Kelly (2007).
** Savery (2015); Gamage & Pang (2003).
*** Anderson (2008).
**** References informing this definition include Battiste (2009); James, Jurich, & Estes (2001); Sinclair, McKendrick, & Scott (2010).
***** Bennis & Nanus (2004); Heckman & Rubinstein (2001).
****** Williams (2005); Hoff (1999).

Using Essential Skills

Successful CFES programs, like those at Milford Central (Box 3.6), incorporate supplemental support for students. The collaborations between and among educators, students, and community members build skills for college and career readiness. This is important because while educational reforms have raised the level of courses required for high school graduation, curriculum is frequently not connected to career readiness (i.e., clusters of related career content), nor does it address the socio-cultural support that empowers low-income students.

Like many student-centered organizations, CFES advocates a particular set of skills. We use this skill set and others in this book because it is crucial that educators and other practitioners in college-access networks understand how student engagement links to the development of skills, their navigation of college and career pathways, and the role of developing new mechanisms for supporting student success.

Conclusion

This chapter provides a three-part framework as a theory of change: organizing, student engagement, and building essential skills. The chapters that follow use the framework to illustrate organizing, student engagement, and students' skill development in diverse settings.

First, organizing for the core practices empowers students to form academic capital for educational and social uplift focusing on organizing school-college networks. The examples show how students who have been

Box 3.6 *Milford Central Weaves CFES into the Curriculum*

Three years ago, Milford Central in Central New York created a class for its CFES mentoring program. When Milford teacher Michael Richtmeier approached the administration at his school about creating a class and granting credit to their CFES mentor/scholars, the administration supported the idea.

It is important to put the right teacher in front of a class like this, and Milford spent a lot of time picking the right one. Ultimately, they settled on a young, enthusiastic teacher whom the students respect and genuinely like—and he was just as excited to work with them. This 1/2-credit class is for high school students in grades 9–12.

The core curriculum of our mentoring class supports the three core practices of CFES: Students work closely with their teacher to learn about college opportunities, and they regularly research college topics, such as how to find a college, visiting colleges, picking a major, and how to pay for college. The students then share this information with their mentees and other students.

The program has grown in response to demand. A second class was added in a year later, and a group of students who had been mentored became mentors themselves. Each class was allowed to play to its strengths: One built a Twitter account to promote good things going on in the building in order to help create a positive school environment.

The other class helped develop Milford's new Backpack program, which provided food for low-income students to take home every weekend, when the school breakfast and lunch programs were idle. Because the CFES program meets regularly as a class—three times every six days—there is adequate time for teachers to work with students on all of the core practices, and for mentors to meet regularly with students as well. The mentoring program is quickly becoming a part of Milford's school culture—as students who were once mentored continue the cycle by becoming mentors, the benefit of CFES becomes clear.

engaged in planning activities centering on the core practices become the agents of change rather than the subjects.

Second, student engagement fuels change. It is crucial for students to engage in core-practice activities. Parents can participate as well, although it is not necessary that they do so. We use student surveys to illustrate patterns of student engagement, but specific activities vary from school to school. Since CFES activities are organized locally—often by students themselves—patterns of engagement vary substantially across sites.

Third, CFES *Essential Skills* help students develop the skills they need to succeed but also provide a means of communicating about socio-cultural outcomes with funding organizations. We do not limit our examples of skills to those adopted by CFES because we realize educators in different states and nations must contend with local standards and policies that emphasize different sets of skills. In this book, our discussions of essential skills highlight how to interpret student comments as evidence of skills development. We encourage educators to use the *CFES Essential Skills*, but also illustrate how core practices relate to skills lists that some schools use in their accountability schemes. This approach can improve communication between practitioners, students, and organizations.

4 | STEM Pathways

Eliseo (Box 4.1) is following the advice that many corporate leaders are offering students: *If you want a job in the new economy, pursue STEM study and skills.* We may not know the jobs of the future, but we do know that most of the high-paying jobs will be STEM-based. The U.S. Department of Labor projects STEM-related jobs will increase by nearly 10 million over the next decade.[1] We present the case for focusing on STEM Pathways, share transferrable organizing strategies that can be widely adapted, and conclude with a brief discussion of career and technical education (CTE) skills.

The Case for STEM Pathways

"Cars that drive themselves, robotic kitchens, manned missions to Mars—this is what our future has in store, and the common thread for these future jobs is STEM," said Kelli Wells, Executive Director of Education and Skills at the GE Foundation, which is committed to closing the skills gap and investing in STEM readiness.

Also in store for our future: An aging population that will require a considerable investment in our nation's healthcare infrastructure. It has been estimated that healthcare comprises the largest segment of workers in the country with "22 million jobs projected by 2022, an increase of five million over the next seven years,"[2] according to Dr. John Fortune, a trauma surgeon at the University of Vermont Medical Center. He created a video on entering the healthcare profession for CFES Scholars.

Fortune recommends that educators use the three Es to move young people toward healthcare professions:

- *Exciting*: Make the study and pursuit of healthcare exciting. Dr. Fortune's video takes students on a roller-coaster ride through a hospital, exposing them to patients who are being admitted while suffering a heart attack.
- *Engaging*: Schedule shadowing experiences for students in local hospitals and provide mentors who are nurses, respiratory therapists, pharmacists, and physical therapists.
- *Experiencing*: Have students learn simple procedures like taking blood pressure, applying a plaster cast, or suturing simulated skin.

To make all of this happen, Fortune urges educators to simply reach out to healthcare providers in their communities and ask. Many hospitals, for example, offer summer "medcamps" and would be happy to open their doors to students, he says.

Techniques such as these could play a pivotal role in encouraging students to pursue degrees not just in healthcare, but in all STEM fields, because despite the fact that students with STEM skills earn significantly more and have lower unemployment rates, STEM degrees make up a relatively small share of all degrees granted in the United States, especially compared to other countries. And only a small proportion of these STEM degrees are awarded to low-income youth.

In the United States, the STEM pipeline for underserved students is broken and the ramifications of this will affect us all. Only six percent of students in the class of 2008 from low-income, high-minority high schools earned an associate, bachelor's, or advanced degree in a STEM field within six years, compared with 17 percent of their higher income peers.[3] Because America's fastest growing cohort consists of low-income children, this trend threatens our nation's economic stability: If we don't provide enough workers for the fast-growing STEM fields, these jobs will go elsewhere.[4] To address this crisis, we must repair the STEM pipeline and dramatically increase the flow of domestic STEM talent from low-income backgrounds. Although this crisis is greater in the United States, Ireland and other Western nations face the same challenge.

Organizing for STEM Pathways

With support from the Helios Foundation, four middle schools in the Tampa Bay area began implementing the CFES STEM program in 2013.[5] In the first year, each school worked with 100 CFES Scholars in grades 6–8. In year two, the program expanded to four high schools, as 8th graders graduated and entered the 9th grade. In year three, two of the middle schools expanded the CFES STEM program to all students, not just a selected number.

Researchers from the University of Michigan conducted qualitative research at two schools in May 2014, Mulberry and Booker Middle Schools. A year later, a researcher from the University of Buffalo conducted an evaluation at three schools: Mulberry and Greco Middle Schools and Mulberry High School.

All CFES Scholars—whether focused on STEM or not—engage in each of the three core practices to help raise their educational aspirations and academic performance. STEM Scholars also participate in activities designed to increase their likelihood of taking STEM courses in high school and college, and ultimately pursue a STEM career.

Pathways

Local, regional, and national college partners play important roles in encouraging students to examine college and careers. The United States Military Academy at West Point (Box 4.2), a national education partner of College For Every Student, brought a traveling robotics workshop to all four of the Florida middle schools; students were inspired by interactions not just with the technology, but also West Point faculty and cadets.

Through the partnership with West Point and other colleges, schools are reporting significant gains in the number of students planning to engage in STEM study and careers. "Among our CFES Scholars, we're seeing a five- to sixfold increase in the number of young people who plan to become engineers, medical doctors and pursue other STEM-connected fields," said Chris Pettit, science teacher and CFES liaison at Greco Middle School in Florida.

Early exposure to college through campus visits—as early as the 6th grade, if not sooner—is critical to producing students who want to pursue STEM study and jobs. Young people who get on college campuses begin to envision themselves as college students. Students in each of the CFES STEM schools spoke of their visits to the University of South Florida, Rollins College, Polk State, and the United States Military Academy at West Point. In these visits, CFES Scholars met with college students who were pursuing STEM majors, visited science labs, and talked with older peers about possible careers and what it takes to become a nurse or a marine biologist.

Just having a willing partner isn't enough to build a successful STEM program. Consider Greco Middle School: Though it is within walking distance of the University of South Florida, which provided both college mentors and on-campus STEM programs, Greco faced challenges securing parental permission for their children to visit colleges, managing the schedules of students, and other logistical issues in getting their students on college campuses. These are common challenges. Resource 4.1 offers creative approaches to expose students to college and suggestions to maximize the STEM impact of visits.

Box 4.2 *West Point: Building Bridges to STEM Readiness*

Since 2013, the United States Military Academy at West Point has worked with CFES to expose CFES Scholars to STEM (see Box 4.1). Over that time, hundreds of middle-school students have participated in mobile robotics workshops led by mathematics professor Dr. Kendall Williams. At these workshops, students assemble and program robots with the help of West Point professors and cadets. In the late spring, West Point opens its doors to CFES students; the academy offers a three-day workshop for 6th and 7th graders who experience life on campus and participate in STEM classes and activities while being mentored by cadets.

Recently, CFES signed an agreement with West Point that will greatly expand STEM opportunities for CFES Scholars, on-campus experiences for high school students, leadership training, and paid STEM internships through the Army Research Labs.

Dr. Donald Outing, the Academy's Chief Diversity Officer, says West Point is committed to building bridges to STEM readiness for students because so much of what the Army does requires technical and scientific expertise. "Here at West Point, we have a responsibility to address this issue of diversity within STEM—to focus our efforts on underrepresented students and to foster an inclusionary and diverse STEM pipeline," Dr. Outing said. "And in doing this, we'll enhance the education and development of all cadets."

Resource 4.1 *Tips for Educators: Exposing Students to College*

Connect college visits to classroom curriculum
Exposure to a science experiment on a college campus can demonstrate how interesting and engaging chemistry or physics can be, especially when younger students see their older peers excited.

"CSI," the long-running crime-lab series on CBS, inspired countless students to pursue forensic science. So when a biology professor at Elmira College in Elmira, N.Y. developed an on-campus science project for middle school students in central New York, she turned to that tried-and-true formula.

The resulting "Way Cool Science" project gave students the opportunity to be part of a college research team, use technology to analyze a mock crime scene, use knowledge of biology, chemistry and physics to figure out what happened and be mentored by undergraduate college students throughout the day.

Use college visits as an incentive

Educators have found success in rewarding students with college visits based on classroom achievements and improved performance. Framing college as a reward for their hard work puts postsecondary education in a positive light.

Elementary school students from Waimanalo, Hawaii, who made the honor roll were invited—along with their families—to a formal celebration hosted by nearby community college. While on campus, students and their families were treated to live music, listened to guest speakers talk about STEM-based middle skill jobs, and received achievement certificates.

Use technology in the classroom to connect students to colleges and careers

Bringing guest speakers to campus can be incredibly valuable, though arranging the logistics can be challenging. Technology can expose students to college and career pathways virtually. Using Skype, FaceTime or other platforms, students can connect with mentors, peek into a college classroom, or tour a college campus anywhere in the world.

Barbara Morgan, a former astronaut and a member of the Teacher in Space Project, spoke about her career with Florida middle school students via Skype. And college students enrolled in a Psychology of Personality course at Chaminade University (Honolulu, Hawaii) served as "e-mentors" to the 7th and 8th graders at New York's Crown Point Central School, 6,000 miles away. Both college-aged and middle school students benefited from these monitored email exchanges.

One way to bring a critical mass of STEM college and career leaders to your school is to host a fair. Fairs provide a great way for students and families to get information about different colleges and careers. In planning these fairs, consider these steps:

- Establish a college and career fair planning committee that includes students and families, along with educators.

- Have students contact colleges and STEM professionals. Work with students to develop a brief script about information they will collect from STEM experts that will later be distributed to fair attendees.

- Promote the college and career fair at school events, on your website, and through social media.

- Invite alumni who are pursuing STEM careers. They bring an important perspective to your students.

- Send formal invitations to students and their families about three weeks before the fair. If you are collaborating with other schools, use community resources to get the word out.

- Provide a directory for students and families that lists each college and STEM professional in attendance and where each can be found at the fair.

- Provide a description of each participating college, including size, location, and popular majors. Ask STEM professionals to list their hiring requirements (college majors and/or coursework).

- Distribute a list of questions students and their families can ask at the fair.

Chapter 2 discussed the mounting challenges students and families face in paying for college. Although there is a growing need for college graduates, the amount of state and federal aid for higher education has not kept pace with college costs. As a result, middle- and low-income students—including those pursuing STEM study—are finding scholarships an increasingly important source of financial aid.

Recognizing the need to build a workforce that reflects current demographics, corporations offer scholarships to encourage more women and people of color to pursue degrees. Box 4.3 provides tips on paying for

Box 4.3 *Finding Dollars to Pay for College*

"If you are going to college, let me hear you make some noise," announced Principal LaShawn Frost of Booker Middle School in Sarasota, Florida, to an auditorium of 120 College For Every Student STEM Scholars. The students erupted with chants and screams.

Director of Financial Aid at Rollins College, Steve Booker, took the stage and offered advice including, "get good grades; work hard; take calculus, physics, and other STEM courses."

The financial aid director went on to suggest that students "be savvy about researching financial aid opportunities online. Do it with your friends. Do it often."

Here are three "paying for college" tips for students as they begin the financial aid process:

1. Don't wait until grade 12. Research scholarships now!

2. Complete the Free Application For Federal Student Aid (FAFSA) (https://fafsa.ed.gov) in January of grade 12. Your parent/guardian should complete their taxes as soon as possible as this information is needed to complete the FAFSA. Resources for FAFSA completion can be found at: https://studentaid.ed.gov/sa/

3. If you have questions after you receive your financial aid package from a college, contact the financial aid office on campus. They are there to help you!

college and shares the sort of activities students can participate in during middle and high schools.

Steve Booker (Box 4.3) reinforces points made in Chapter 2. College is often expensive (a point also made in Chapter 3), so students need to learn about paying-for-college strategies early, and they need to understand requirements like the FAFSA. It is never too early for students and families to begin looking for resources. Encourage students to conduct online searches and ask college students, professors, and STEM professionals about scholarships. Resource 4.2 provides a worksheet designed to help students organize scholarship leads.

Resource 4.2 *STEM Scholarship Search*

Note the following details about each scholarship you find to help organize your search and application process:

Name of scholarship:_____

Scholarship provider:_____

Application deadline:_____

Potential amount ($):_____

Scholarship requirements:

- Essay
- Transcript
- Letter of recommendation
- Interview
- Other

What makes you a competitive applicant for this scholarship?
_____
_____

What do you need to strengthen academics, extracurricular involvement, leadership, etc.? What can you do to ensure that you achieve these gains?
_____
_____

Mentoring

College students studying in STEM fields and professionals with STEM jobs can make ideal mentors and role models for students. Jasmine, a former CFES Scholar who graduated from Booker High School and University of South Florida (USF) and recently entered medical school, organized mentoring by college students for all four Florida middle schools in the CFES STEM program. Each mentor was majoring in a STEM subject, such as pre-med or chemistry. Distance from USF became a factor for Mulberry and Booker's mentors. Because of a 90-minute drive each way, these mentors were not able to visit as frequently as they and the Scholars wanted. So the schools tapped into nearby colleges for mentors. Booker found mentors at New College, and Mulberry began working with Florida Southern.

Jasmine also created Science For Every Student, a daylong program in the early spring that brought 100 CFES Scholars from the four middle schools to the USF campus. Two years later, that event grew to include more than 500 CFES Scholars from middle and high schools. During Science For Every Student day, students attend science classes, learn about research from college professors and participate in science experiments with USF students.

In reviewing the CFES STEM program, the University of Buffalo evaluator noted that schools were using four different forms of mentoring— peer mentoring (high school students with middle school students); college students mentoring middle and high school students; teacher-led mentoring groups; and schoolwide programs that brought professionals into the school to discuss their careers.

Mulberry uses a hybrid mentoring model that involves peers, older students, teachers, and corporate leaders. Each Mulberry student is part of a group of ten peers that gathers at least twice monthly to discuss aspirations and anything that they feel may be standing in the way of their goals. Each of these groups names itself, often after a college. Dani Torres, who serves as the migrant advocate in the Mulberry schools, mentioned a team who called themselves the "Harvard Hopefuls" after a Mulberry grad who is now a student at Harvard. "They all aspire to be like him," said Torres, who with nine other Mulberry educators met with their student teams twice each month. Mulberry also hosts events where parents and community members share their career paths.

Corporate partners, too, provide mentors. Kelly Larrow, who coordinates the CFES STEM program at Mulberry and teaches science, was able to forge an alliance with FedEx after learning the company was having difficulty introducing a computer science curriculum into local schools. "When I described the CFES program and the Scholars they could reach, they were thrilled to see that we already had that framework in place for them to plug into," Larrow said. "We're now in our second year of partnership with them and the program has grown from a single-semester class taught once a week by computer scientists from FedEx to a full-year curriculum including programming, robotics, and code writing that also includes a feeder elementary school." Since FedEx faces a shortage of code writers, this sort of win–win relationship can be established in schools across the United States and beyond.

Many mentoring programs incorporate tutoring in STEM subjects. Building a successful STEM tutoring program into your school can incorporate all three CFES core practices (Leadership Through Service, Mentoring, and Pathways to College and Career). Whether you have a teacher-led, college student-led, or peer-led model, your students will increase their STEM confidence and skills. Resource 4.3 offers strategies to consider as you design and implement a STEM tutoring program.

Leadership Through Service

Students who serve as mentors engage in Leadership Through Service. When they work with younger students, mentors benefit, too, as they and their mentees learn collaboratively and develop team building skills.

Some examples of service and leadership development activities in the Florida CFES STEM schools:

- At Mulberry Middle, student groups planned and implemented a cleanup for community centers, beautified community parks, and tutored younger students in math and science.
- At Booker Middle, students started a recycling club and tutored elementary school students in math and science.
- Mulberry High Scholars recruited 40 professionals to come into the school to discuss their STEM careers. Every classroom had two visitors, and their goal was to give all students access to knowledge about college and career.
- Andy Ng, a former CFES Scholar at Booker High School, NYU graduate and current Google employee, spoke about leadership, college goals, and college knowledge at the eight Florida schools.

Resource 4.3 *STEM Mentors become Tutors*

- *Keep student-to-tutor ratios low*: Provide students with one-on-one tutoring or groups no larger than five students to one tutor. Students need personal attention to master content; keeping the ratio low allows tutors to provide attention to individual students.

- *Train your tutors*: Whether you have teachers, STEM professionals, college students, or older peers, provide training so that the tutors know what to expect. Training should cover basic tutoring techniques and address questions or concerns tutors may have.

- *Set goals, and reward tutees when they meet goals*: Students will be motivated if they have attainable goals, and if there is incentive for reaching those goals. Provide incentives donated by local businesses and organizations. Businesses are often excited to partner with their local schools, so don't be afraid to ask!

- *Make tutoring more than just "homework help"*: Tutoring sessions can develop and strengthen content knowledge, as well as mentoring and help build the *Essential Skills* such as grit, teamwork, and leadership.

- *Keep a consistent schedule*: Keep the tutoring schedule and tutors consistent—having the same tutor each day or week allows the tutees to build stronger relationships.

- *Make tutoring fun!*: Students may be struggling with a specific STEM concept. Inherently, this struggle can breed frustration, so keep the tutoring sessions fun, engaging, and encouraging! Some programs release mentors and mentees early to shoot baskets in the gym or provide occasional ice cream socials.

Box 4.4 is an example of how high school students can mentor younger peers in science. Service activities provide myriad ways for Scholars to enhance STEM learning that benefits mentors and mentees.

Box 4.4 *Scholars Teach Science to Younger Peers**

At Booker High School, CFES Scholar leaders reviewed, assembled, organized and executed science experiments with elementary school students. Each science experiment included a description, discussion points, and work items needed to complete the experiment.

The younger students were challenged to develop ideas/ hypotheses regarding how and why these experiments worked. For each experiment, students completed knowledge cards with an explanation of the scientific facts underlying the experiment, using scientific vocabulary and providing definitions. CFES Scholars led younger students in methods for organizing their thoughts and conclusions regarding the scientific principles at work in each experiment. CFES Scholar leaders also assisted the younger students in researching additional facts (utilizing library resources) between sessions and sharing those facts with each class session.

CFES Scholar leaders:

- demonstrated enhanced leadership skills,
- gained service hours,
- added to their résumés, and
- created awareness in STEM related areas.

Elementary students:

- gained greater understanding, interest, and exposure to STEM subject matter;
- enhanced literacy in science terms, knowledge, and content;
- enhanced skill development in critical thinking, problem solving, time management, writing, teamwork, and presentations, thus building self confidence; and
- developed the Essential Skills

* This activity was organized and led by Ted Downing, a community volunteer from Sarasota, Florida.

Students who demonstrate aptitude for technology and the sciences can be given an outlet for those passions that incorporates Leadership Through Service. At Cloonan Middle School in Stamford, CT, for example, a CFES STEM Scholar designed a project that melds service and his passion, working with computers.

Box 4.5 *Connecticut 8th Grader Changing Students' Lives, One Hard Drive at a Time**

One of the hardest working information technology people at Connecticut's Cloonan Middle School is an 8th grader named Daniel, who is part of the College For Every Student STEM program.

Over a year ago, assistant principal Laureen Mody commissioned Daniel to "clean" old computers and install new operating systems onto them. The computers are then given to students for use at home.

Mody calls Daniel a role model, a leader, and a tremendous asset to Cloonan's CFES team. "He is a computer whiz and a wonderful person," said Mody. "What he does for his fellow students is life-changing."

Daniel doesn't just work on computers because he is good at it—he works on them because he knows that his peers rely on these computers for their education. "It's a great feeling to give my classmates a way to study and further themselves at home," said Daniel. "I help them because it's what I love to do."

"CFES makes me a better person all around," he said. "I attended the leadership workshop in New York City last year and it helped me get out of my comfort zone. I now use that experience to help me communicate with people."**

* Most of this piece was taken from an article in the *Stamford Daily Voice* (March 3, 2015).

** As a high school student, Daniel returns to Cloonan Middle School regularly to train the student Tech Team that is following in his footsteps by reformatting and updating donated laptops for their peers to use.

Internships

Middle and high schools benefit from external support that helps them prepare their students for college and careers, especially since educators may not have the time to find or access to networks that can link them with college and career partners and provide STEM resources.

Participating in a STEM internship, for example, yields multiple benefits. Internships provide not only the opportunity for CFES STEM Scholars to gain valuable insights into STEM fields, but also for them to apply their leadership skills and develop into young professionals. STEM internships also enhance résumés and college applications. Resource 4.4 provides some steps educators can encourage their students to take to find an appropriate internship.

Resource 4.4 *An Outline of Steps Educators Can Encourage Students to Take to Find and Secure a STEM Internship*

Define your interests

Brainstorm a list of questions: *What is my dream job? What kind of internship can help me develop my skills?* If you are interested in the medical field, for example, don't limit yourself to only looking for internships at hospitals—think about community clinics that serve the homeless, pharmaceutical companies, or home healthcare product companies. STEM fields are interconnected, so even if you find an internship that is not exactly in line with what you ultimately hope to do, it will still give you insight into the field, and may help you further define your interests.

Do research

Once you've defined potential areas of interest, do some research. Find out what local companies and organizations exist within that interest area. Visit their websites and contact them to inquire about internship opportunities. Reach out to your network—mentors, teachers, community leaders—and seek information from them.

They can help you find internship opportunities and prepare materials you will need as a competitive applicant for internships.

Write and edit your résumé

List your skills and extracurricular activities. Use an online résumé template to organize your information. Be specific and include data and/or results. For example, "Increased the number of students attending after school math tutoring from 10 to 35 by personally reaching out to math teachers to target at-risk students." Ask your mentor or teacher to proofread your résumé.

Be informed

Learn about the organization. You don't need to know its whole history or every detail, but you want to know what it does and what its goals are. This information can be found on the organization's website.

Write and edit your cover letter

A cover letter must accompany your résumé. This letter should express your interests and goals relevant to the organization. Demonstrate your written communication skills. Review your letter multiple times and ask someone to proofread it. Personalize your letter by putting an inside address for the organization and the name of the hiring manager at the top.

Ace the interview

Be prepared, dress appropriately, and arrive early. Convey your confidence and knowledge by asking relevant questions and expressing your interest in the organization. Follow up immediately with a formal thank you note.

Conclusion

Given the renewed emphasis on STEM pathways, it is important to work with local employers and student advocates to create visibility into emerging career pathways. As we noted in Chapter 2, technology is now integral to most professions, from the arts through science and engineering.

School–college–community networks can use the core practices to encourage students to explore new options and opportunities. We further explore and illuminate strategies for integrating an emphasis on technology into preparation and career readiness in all fields, not just science and engineering.

5 Urban Schools

Box 5.1 *Urban Hope and Inspiration*

During his sophomore year at Seward Park High School in lower Manhattan, Angel sat in detention because he had brought a knife to school—something he admitted was "stupid." He ruminated on his future. Would he drop out of high school like his older sister? Or was there something more for him? As he idled, Angel heard students in the hallway. They talked about visiting colleges and pursuing careers.

The Seward Park principal had seen something in Angel, and she approached him about joining the program that met after school. "Sure, why not?" Angel said. He attended his first CFES meeting the next day.

"I visited colleges," Angel said. "I met college students. They were role models and leaders. I had a chance to practice my own leadership skills. I became a positive role model." Three years later, Angel entered the State University of New York at Plattsburgh, where he became student body president in his senior year. A year later, he completed a master's degree at Plattsburgh.

Throughout his college career, Angel stayed connected to CFES. He spoke at CFES conferences and other events and mentored younger students. Eventually, CFES offered Angel a position as a program director in New York City schools and in other regions, including a Native American school in North Dakota. In his sixth year as a CFES professional, helping urban youth get on a better path, Angel entered a doctoral program at Columbia's Teachers College.

College For Every Student has helped thousands of students like Angel overcome the tyranny of low expectations. Most students in urban areas, though, never get the chance to excel. Close to half the students in large urban districts[1] across the United States drop out of high school.[2]

This starts with a look at challenges faced by urban educators and some of the solutions they employ. Given the troubling trends toward inequalities for urban students compared to peers in suburban schools, we encourage you to use core practices to overcome barriers facing many low-income students as they move toward college and career readiness. Partnerships with colleges and businesses, as well as collaborations with rural schools and other strategies, offer innovative and practical ways to benefit urban schools and students. Using these strategies empowers urban educators to provide opportunities for their students to build the *Essential Skills.*

Organizing in Urban Schools

A recent report, *Framing Urban School Challenges,*[3] identified several significant obstacles facing urban schools:

- high concentrations of poverty
- racial and ethnic diversity
- large concentrations of immigrant populations and linguistic diversity
- frequent turnover as students move from school to school.

Having worked with 500 urban and 300 rural schools, CFES knows that these four challenges, as well as many others, are not unique to urban areas. The unemployment rate on the rural Standing Rock Sioux Reservation, South Dakota, for example, where CFES has worked for five years, is more than 60 percent.[4] At Mulberry Middle and High Schools in Florida (Chapter 4), both part of CFES, more than 20 percent of the students are children of migrant workers who pick oranges and strawberries seasonally; they move in and out of school often, shuttling between Mexico and farms in Florida and other states. Many of the shared practical strategies in this chapter can be applied to rural schools as well.

Not all challenges faced by urban and rural schools, though, are the same. Just as schools in rural areas must overcome the provincial attitudes that come from relative isolation (Chapter 6), greater population density causes its own problems.

In addition to the challenges already listed, urban schools are faced with significant educational inequality between the haves and have-nots. "The reality of educational opportunity has become that those who can afford it—either through higher property taxes in suburbs or by paying tuition for elite private schools—have better access to higher-quality college preparatory education than poor and working-class families living in neighborhoods in American cities with large concentrations of poverty," Ed St. John and his research team wrote in *Left Behind: Urban High Schools and the Failure of Market Reform*.[5] Market mechanisms have done little to reduce these inequalities in American cities. For example, school-choice schemes and themed high schools leave many low-income students behind because, as we discuss later in this chapter, they are uninformed consumers and they don't know how, nor have they been shown how, to navigate the maze. Thus, they are often trapped in schools that have been unable to improve.[6] Attempts to level the playing field in urban communities have instead tilted schools toward greater inequality.

These inequalities have become more intractable as two conflicting policy trajectories in urban school districts—standards and markets—have converged. Standards-driven reforms were framed as a national response to global economic competition. As these reforms evolved, urban school districts implemented wave after wave of changes to comply with an ever-lengthening set of imperatives. In its most recent iteration, the standards movement focuses on both college preparatory courses *and* career-oriented content, often with an emphasis on technical education in STEM fields.[7]

At the same time, a so-called urban market strategy unfolded in many areas, under which schools compete with one another for students. As promoted by John Chubb and Terry Moe's *Politics, Markets, and America's Schools*,[8] a study of New York City schools, markets were touted as a mechanism for improving educational outcomes in urban schools. The artifacts of this blueprint for urban school reform include charter schools, which compete with public schools (who are also competing with each other) for students in most cities. Because charter laws exempt these schools from the control of school districts, two types of schools were created—one with the freedom to innovate (the charter schools), the other (traditional public schools) with embedded constraints on their curriculum—but neither type outperformed the other on educational outcomes.[9]

Urban Schools in Transformation

Many urban school systems that once funneled students into large, comprehensive high schools have already shifted their approach. Today, these districts have splintered into smaller schools or have established small academies within larger schools.[10] These academies are focused on themes driven by market forces and promote in-demand college majors and careers. Their overriding goal is to prepare students for technical careers and basic collegiate work upon graduation from high school.

In theory, the re-formed, urban-education market system would give students background they need to enter the 21st-century workforce. In reality, though, low-income families are at a competitive disadvantage in navigating these urban educational systems, and they never realize the expected gains. Often, families don't know how to move through the complicated market-driven maze known as school choice, and their children pay the price. Low-income families are less likely to understand the bureaucracies, practices, and complexities of schools and colleges. Middle school students and families have limited support when choosing a high school. Students who decide to attend a specialized high school may be shaping their major, college choice, and career opportunities at the age of 13 without understanding future implications.

Urban students face other challenges, too. Despite coming from places with vast cultural, entertainment, and other opportunities at their doorsteps, urban students are often as isolated as their rural counterparts. Many students who live in the Bronx, for instance, have never been to Wall Street, just a subway ride away. In fact, according to one principal at a CFES school in the South Bronx, "these young people are more likely to visit relatives in the Dominican Republic than enter lower Manhattan."

On the other hand, urban schools have some built-in advantages. While the students are often cloistered, urban students, unlike their rural peers, have more proximate opportunities to expand their horizons. Marta Valle High School on the Lower East Side of Manhattan, for example, has three colleges, eight museums, and countless cultural opportunities within one mile of school.

CFES has found that our rural students are often less adventurous than their urban peers. Each summer, CFES offers three-day residential college experiences for rising high school seniors known as College Explore. This program, staffed by college admissions directors and CFES professionals, is free for CFES Scholars, both urban and rural, but urban students participate at a rate six times higher than their rural peers. "Rural kids are less likely to see themselves as leaders and step outside their comfort zones than their urban peers," one superintendent said.

Facing the New Challenges

The *Plattsburgh Press-Republican* captured this spirit of exploration in an article about an exchange that brought Harlem students to Willsboro, NY, a rural community on the western shore of Lake Champlain in the Adirondacks (Box 5.2).

Box 5.2 *City Teens Uncowed by Rural Visit**

The experiences of city and country teens are often worlds apart.

"I can't believe I touched a cow," Isaiah exclaimed during a recent visit to the Lee Garvey Farm in Willsboro. "I can't process that in my brain."

A group of students and educators from Wadleigh Secondary School and Frederick Douglass Academy II in New York City visited the North Country as Scholars with College For Every Student.

They watched the farmer milk the cows.

The walk through the cow barn was eye-popping.

"Oh, my God, that is the weirdest thing," one student called out. "[That cow's] tongue is so huge!"

A bat darted through the barn, and the startled visitors pulled their jackets over their heads—at first, they thought it was a bird.

Then the scholars were treated to farm-fresh apples, cheese and apple cider.

"They seem to be having a grand time coming here to see the cows," Moran said.

This was the sixth year Willsboro Central School hosted New York City students through College For Every Student's Exchange Program.

"Our kids look forward to this all year," said teacher Marie Blatchley. "They enjoy both hosting the New York City students and then getting the opportunity to visit their schools a few days later."

The students from the city welcomed the opportunity to see rural life, but the visit raised some questions about wide-open spaces.

"How do people handle it?" Ariely wondered. "Everything is so far away, while everything is so close in the city."

Classmate Julissa, who is looking into industrial engineering, echoed some of the same sentiments.

"The city is a different world," she said. "Looking at this experience, upstate is a very big neighborhood. It surprised me that every grade has only about 15 kids."

Part of the North Country visit focused on exposing the high-school students to a variety of college campuses.

College For Every Student Program Director Leroy Nesbitt led a financial-aid workshop at Willsboro Central School. Then the students visited Clinton Community College and SUNY Plattsburgh for campus tours and a career-guidance workshop.

"I am a shy person, so maybe this experience will get me out of my shell," Theresa said of her visit to the North Country.

"I hope to major in the field of business. I think it is important to get out and meet new people and get connections."

The CFES scholars from both Willsboro and New York City also collaborated on a jointly planned service project—they delivered flowers in personalized, hand-painted terracotta pots to a local senior citizens center.

A group of Willsboro students then traveled to New York City to experience life from an urban perspective.

Teams of College For Every Student scholars from around the city met at the Apollo Theater in Harlem for the CFES Student Leadership Summit, a scholar-directed event designed to build and strengthen leadership skills and emphasize the important role they play in college and career success.

The Willsboro scholars and their New York City peers wrapped up their exchange with a visit to Columbia University.

"Our students will come away from the exchange with new friends and new perspectives on being a young adult," Willsboro Superintendent Steve Broadwell said before the trip.

"They will have a better understanding of life in the city and the challenges of city life, as well as the benefits of living in (New York City)."

* Article in the *Plattsburgh Press-Republican* (June 19, 2013) by Alvin Reiner.

Urban–rural school-to-school partnerships can open up new worlds for students and prepare them for the diversity they will see in college. School–college partnerships are more common; these partnerships are usually between institutions in a 75-mile radius, though some are further away. Middlebury College in Vermont and DeWitt Clinton High School in the Bronx, for example, are almost 300 miles apart. *To Share A Dream*, a monograph written about that partnership, articulates the value of the diversity it provides: "The differences between Middlebury and DeWitt Clinton strengthen their relationship. The institutions are so different that their interaction forces students and teachers to re-examine their own values and directions. The difference provides a 'jump start to learning . . .'"[11]

The most comprehensive of these long-distance partnerships is the one between the University of Vermont and Christopher Columbus High School in the Bronx (Box 5.3), which has flourished for nearly two decades.

As beneficial as partnerships can be to both institutions in the relationship, they can't guarantee that all students will be successful. They take time to build, effort to nurture once established, and, above all, require focus and direction. Over the years, CFES has observed these characteristics of successful school–college partnerships:

1. *Partnerships need a champion.* At Christopher Columbus, the principal, Gerald Garfin, was fully committed to the partnerships' success. Garfin

Box 5.3 *Unlikely Partners Find Common Ground*

In 2000, shortly after becoming the principal at Christopher Columbus High School in the Bronx, Jerry Garfin told the President of CFES, Rick Dalton, "I want Columbus to regain its glory and become the best school in the Bronx. I went to this school. I love this place."

Garfin asked Dalton if CFES could help him find a college partner. "It's part of my vision," said Garfin. Through a former board member at the University of Vermont (UVM), Richard Tarrant, Dalton was able to get the attention of the UVM provost who asked his admissions director, Don Honeman, to attend a CFES workshop in Mount Kisco, NY.

At the workshop, Garfin and Honeman sketched out the first steps in a plan that would change the destinies of both institutions and ultimately hundreds of low-income students from the Bronx. JetBlue Airlines joined the partnership by providing 300 free round-trip tickets each year between New York and Burlington, VT. "That reduced the distance between us. Instead of five hours of travel, we were 60 minutes apart," said Garfin. This enabled students and staff to visit the University of Vermont and members of the UVM faculty and staff to visit the Columbus campus in the Bronx.

Over the last decade and a half, more than 280 young people from Columbus High School, and the two small schools that were created in the building after the partnership was established, Collegiate Institute for Math and Science and Pelham Preparatory Academy, have attended the University of Vermont. A staggering 80 percent of those students have attained UVM degrees or are on target to do so, and scholarships and support from UVM totals more than $30 million.

The partnership has been marked by myriad activities centered on college pathway knowledge, mentoring, *Essential Skills*, and academic enrichment. Columbus students in grades 9–12 receive extensive support in understanding college pathways from UVM admissions and financial aid officers who meet with them in the Bronx and Vermont. There are summer internships for Columbus students at UVM; students from UVM teach at Columbus; UVM professors teach high school English and science; college and high school students perform service activities side-by-side; and the UVM choir and vocal groups perform for Columbus families and in the school's hallways.

Each year, according to Garfin, several hundred educators and students from both institutions participate in and benefit from the partnership.

realized that he needed to market the partnership in his building and neighborhood and needed to be responsive to his Vermont partners. "When they called with a question or a request, I got back to them within the hour," he said. Projects that thrive are led by individuals who consider them vitally important or other responsibilities will supersede them.

2. *Partnerships must meet the needs of both institutions.* The University of Vermont, located in one of the whitest states in the country, desperately wanted diversity, while Columbus, in its quest to become the top high school in the Bronx, saw how a college partner could boost its academics, reputation, and schoolwide college readiness.

3. *Partnerships need clear goals and agreed upon timelines.* Early each fall, a team from both Columbus and UVM create an annual plan that guides activities throughout the year.

4. *Top leaders need to buy in.* Garfin visited UVM two or three times each year to meet with key college leaders and Columbus students that had matriculated there. UVM's president also visited Columbus regularly.

5. *Develop a team.* Partnerships that are led and implemented by one person don't survive. Individuals get burned out; individuals leave. Several people at both Columbus High School (including teachers, an administrator, and community leaders) and the University of Vermont (the admissions dean, administrators, professors) served as de facto team members, helping to develop, market, and implement the plan. A successful partnership requires significant resources, the most important of which is personnel time, to succeed.

6. *Think outside the box.* Columbus 9th graders completed a sample college application and wrote college essays that were then reviewed by admissions directors from UVM. Each year the admissions team

selected the 15 best applications; these students visited UVM for an overnight stay, during which they toured the campus, attended classes, and met with former Columbus students now attending UVM.

These partnerships are valuable, but they require special care (Box 5.4). For example, the Middlebury College–DeWitt Clinton High School partnership got off to a robust start when eight Middlebury professors spent the day at Clinton teaching classes.

Box 5.4 *An Education for Us**

On a cold, windswept February day in the Bronx, eight Middlebury College faculty members walk up the marble steps, past the Corinthian columns and through the front doors of DeWitt Clinton to begin the first "Middlebury Day."

Minutes later, as they enter the principal's office, they are warmly greeted by David Fuchs.

"Have a cup of coffee, a bagel," he says.

When the clock strikes 8:30, the Middlebury professors nervously trudge off with student hosts to several classrooms. In Dan Kaplan's physics class, Prof. Bob Prigo explains how Newton's laws can help students swish basketballs. Then, just as the bell rings, with a drum roll behind him, Prigo applies Newton's laws by breaking four pine boards with his fist to the delight of his physics class. Perhaps it is this moment, accentuated by the laughter and applause of the students, that signals "yes," the partnership can work. Fears about unreachable students and distant faculty vanish.

These eight faculty members return to Middlebury with new images of the inner-city high school. Rich Wolfson, a physics professor, recalls the day he spent teaching at Clinton: "I remember walking the halls between classes and peering into classrooms. After all one has heard about chaos in inner-city schools, I was surprised at how quiet it was and how studious-looking each class was. It's been an education for us that things may not be as hopeless as the media make them seem."

This visit was a first step, a test. It allowed both DeWitt Clinton and Middlebury to see whether or not they could—and would—proceed further. "It just clicked," says Ron Nief, Middlebury's Director of Public Affairs. The initial day in the Bronx, according to DeWitt Clinton's Marlene Buckley, "let DeWitt Clinton see that Middlebury faculty weren't condescending and, in turn, let Middlebury see that we had plenty of bright, caring kids and teachers."

The success of the first Middlebury Day won the support of the Middlebury College community. The stereotype of the inner-city school had been broken for many of the visiting faculty. Provost John McCardell, who taught several history classes at DeWitt Clinton, reported to the president's cabinet in glowing terms. A few days later, Middlebury President Olin Robinson pledged his support to the Partnership, and that April, Robinson and Fuchs officially announced the Partnership's formation at a media-filled ceremony at DeWitt Clinton.

* Dalton (1990).

Some of the most memorable lessons students learn are about college and career pathways, and lifestyles that differ from their own. The *Essential Skills*, derived from working within these partnerships, expand opportunity. Urban schools have an advantage over their rural counterparts in this department also: Partners are simply easier to find in urban areas, where there are myriad colleges, businesses and nonprofit groups. Urban CFES schools have developed partnerships with financial service corporations like Goldman Sachs, other schools, and law firms like Schulte Roth & Zabel in Manhattan (Box 5.5).

Engagement: Core Practices in Action

The best partnerships, such as this one between a law firm and an urban school (Box 5.5), incorporate all three CFES core practices:

1. *Pathways*—Students learned about legal careers by meeting with attorneys in a Manhattan law office, and they also received general college advice.

> ## Box 5.5 *NYC Lawyers Mentor Bronx Students*
>
> Attorneys from the midtown Manhattan office of Schulte Roth & Zabel LLP (SRZ) hosted a three-event seminar titled CLASS (College, Leadership & Success Seminars) for 20 CFES Scholars from Eximius College Preparatory Academy in the Bronx. The goal of the day-long event: For students to hone their public speaking, networking, and leadership skills.
>
> At the first seminar, each student was given a packet with handouts, relevant articles and agendas. CFES Scholars and SRZ mentors discussed college and career readiness strategies, addressing topics such as professional etiquette, goal setting, and the college search process.
>
> During the last seminar, several lawyers and other legal professionals discussed legal careers. Scholars spent one-on-one time networking with panelists and learned about the many careers they could pursue in law: Trial lawyer, family law attorney, paralegal, court administration careers.

2. *Mentoring*—Three attorneys in the firm mentored 20 high school students during the three seminars.

3. *Leadership Through Service*—High school students were exposed to young attorneys who exhibited exemplary leadership skills by taking on and implementing the partnership. The students experienced firsthand the value of service.

Multiple Mentoring Models

External mentors, such as the lawyers from Manhattan and the students from the University of Vermont, are important—they bring a perspective that students, cloistered in their own communities, frequently are not exposed to. Having mentors close to home can be powerful, though—and you can often find them inside your own school.

Peer mentors give Scholars living proof that others have encountered and overcome the same issues they have faced (Box 5.6). Together, Scholars and their peer mentors put together plans to surmount academic and social difficulties, yielding rewards for both. "When I first met my mentee, she'd been failing most of her classes," one mentor said. "I told her we were going to set days to study for certain classes so she could build her grades up, one-by-one, in each class. When she told me she got an A in one of her classes and the last report card, it made me feel like I was really making a difference."

Box 5.6 *Teachers and Peers as Mentors in Brooklyn*

Each day, CFES Scholars from Brooklyn Institute for Liberal Arts (BILA) begin their day with a mentoring session. Twenty teachers and counselors serve as mentors for students and meet with their assigned mentees each morning to discuss academics and personal matters.

"Sometimes we play games, and have conversations," said Danielle, a junior at BILA. "It's really a great way to start the school day and gives us a chance to discuss issues or simply just ease into the day."

Along with the daily morning check-in, the mentors create fun, informative, and engaging lessons. For two hours every Wednesday, mentor/mentee pairs gather in groups to talk about topics such as study skills, healthy relationships, bullying, team building, and current events.

"Mentors provide the much-needed support that our students need to flourish by displaying information in an engaging way," said guidance counselor Zaneta George-Cipriani. "Our CFES Scholars have shown increased interest in taking leadership roles and have taken initiative to become change agents in their school and community."

Danielle is just one Scholar who has grown through her involvement with CFES and as a result became BILA's first National Honor Society President. "I have always been a determined student, but my involvement with CFES has helped me hone my communication skills and step up as a leader."

As a member of the CFES leadership team, Danielle attended the CFES National Conference last fall and used the opportunity for her own professional development.

"I really enjoyed being part of the CFES Leadership team," Danielle stated. "I found myself taking initiative in service projects and organizing events at school."

According to George-Cipriani, Danielle's classmate Tracy was also "inspired into action" by CFES and created a peer-tutoring program.

"15 juniors tutor freshmen and sophomores during the lunch period," Tracy said. "We help students in all subject areas and the teachers have told us that students' grades have improved and the tutoring has helped prepare them for Regents exams."

College For Every Student has one of the most extensive peer mentoring programs in the world. Each year, more than 20,000 CFES Scholars in grades K-12 participate in peer mentoring. It works because of the unique bond formed between students and mentors. While most mentors and mentees become friends, these friendships begin in a school-based setting, with conversations designed to inspire a drive for academic and personal excellence among all CFES Scholars—whether they are the mentor or mentee. Equally important, the mentored Scholars know those leading them have faced similar challenges and gained real-life experience that they are happy to discuss (Resource 5.1).

Resource 5.1 *Tips for Establishing Successful Peer Mentor Programs*

Engage students: Peer mentors who help plan their program are more motivated and invested in the program's success, and they often do a better job inspiring and moving their peers into action than adults do. Successful peer mentoring programs require adults who listen and tap into student expertise.

Make it meaningful: Peer mentors want to make a difference. Mentors like to know their work is improving the life of another and, in return, is helping them. Positive feedback to peer mentors contributes to future success.

Build a strong core peer mentoring team: Core teams of peer mentors should meet frequently. Scheduling a common advisory period or study hall is one way of encouraging interaction. Consider engaging more than one or two students on the core team through the CFES Club or student leadership team.

Simplify: Design peer mentoring that engages other CFES core practices. While Castle High School students in Honolulu were cleaning a fish pond with their peer mentees from Dole Middle School, they exhibited leadership qualities, engaged in service, and also had conversations about college pathways with the younger students.

Set calendar early: Help people stay focused by scheduling mentor meetings as soon as possible. Begin building the calendar by establishing program kick-off and wrap-up dates. Then be sure to build in celebrations, mentor check-in meetings, etc.

Provide effective, ongoing training: Peer Mentors need to know what is expected of them and what they can expect from mentoring. Initial mentor training is a must. The most effective training is ongoing: Follow up the initial mentor training by personal check-ins or brief meetings.

Spread good news: Broadcast success and achievements. Don't wait until the end of the school year, start right away. Have peer mentors write articles about mentoring for the school paper. Spread the good news about peer mentoring and create a buzz in the halls.

Leadership Through Service

Service is a two-way street. While students from disadvantaged neighborhoods benefit greatly when others pitch in to show them the way to college, they should do what they can to serve their schools and communities as well. In many urban sites, CFES Scholars plan and implement leadership summits. Each year, for example, Scholars from New York City schools hold a leadership summit at the Apollo Theater, the iconic Harlem landmark. Other leadership summits have been organized by CFES Scholars in dozens of cities, including Denver, Cincinnati, Boston, and Honolulu. At these summits, students recruit panelists, often young professionals who have risen from low income backgrounds to successful positions, to talk about service and leadership. The students themselves lead workshops on topics such as bullying prevention, becoming a better leader, and making the right choices.

Often Leadership Through Service activities focus on helping classmates and younger peers develop college pathway knowledge (Box 5.7). "We go to an elementary school once a month and teach kids about college," one middle school student from Harlem said of his own service. "We do activities with them like face painting. We read to them and we talk about setting goals."

Engagement in leadership opportunities also motivates students to mentor others, as Azeezat's story reveals (Box 5.8).

Box 5.7 Leadership: "I Am in Charge of My Destiny and So Are You"

"Getting involved with College For Every Student was an eye-opening experience for me," said Diamond, a CFES alumna who spoke at the graduation ceremony of her alma mater, Isaac Newton Middle School of Math and Science in Harlem.

Diamond, now in her second year at the University at Albany, remembers joining CFES in the 7th grade. "This was the first time I ever talked about college," she said. "I remember it was like something foreign and intangible. We talked about colleges and what they offered. We learned about choosing majors based on your career interests. It wasn't long before I realized that I could do this 'college thing'."

During her graduation speech, Diamond told students, "CFES was the seed that was implanted in me at a young age and helped me become college and career ready."

Diamond continued to pave her college path throughout high school.

"I was expecting a straight and narrow path, but the truth is, it wasn't," Diamond told the students at the graduation ceremony. "I really wanted to go to Howard University in Washington, DC. It was my dream. I applied and then I got accepted. And then I realized I couldn't afford it. So, I thought about my options and I decided to go to a community college closer to home."

As a first-generation college student, Diamond admits this was a tough decision, but one she believes made all the difference.

"Going to college is not like school. You're there because you chose to be and you're taking courses that you want to take," she told students. "Focus on your schoolwork and get involved. Through my involvement with CFES, I gained leadership skills. It made me realize that I could be independent. It raised my self-esteem. It showed me that *Diamond* was going to take me places," she said, pointing to herself. "Not my mom, not my teachers, but me. I am in charge of my destiny and so are you."

Box 5.8 *CFES Scholar Attends First Lady's "Beating the Odds" Summit*

"To be able to say that I met the First Lady and shook hands with the President is incredible," said Azeezat, a CFES Scholar who graduated from Eximius Preparatory Academy.

Azeezat was one of 140 college-bound students from across the nation invited to the White House for the Reach Higher "Beating the Odds" Summit hosted by the First Lady in the summer of 2015.

"One day I got a text from my advisor that read, 'Do you want to go to the White House?' My first thought was, 'I have to go. I have to get ready.'"

Although she says this experience is the highlight along her pathway to college, Azeezat has always been focused on college. In 10th grade, she became a College For Every Student Scholar and learned about the college process through her CFES mentor.

"Three years later, my mentor and I are still connected," said Azeezat. "He helped me understand the college process. CFES not only expanded my knowledge of college, but added to my enthusiasm for wanting to go to college."

At the end of her sophomore year, Azeezat attended CFES College Explore, a three-day residential experience at Paul Smith's College in New York State's Adirondack Park.

"It was amazing," she exclaimed. "This was the first time I had been out of the city without my parents and in a college environment."

Azeezat and 40 other CFES Scholars lived in college dorms, attended classes taught by college professors, participated in admissions and financial aid workshops, learned college interview and essay writing skills, and took part in leadership activities.

"It was nice to see first-hand what college would be like. I didn't want to leave. The whole experience was fun and informative and that is where I started my network and really honed my communication skills," she added.

With this experience under her belt, Azeezat was fortified for her junior year.

"I became a CFES mentor," she stated. "I attended a peer mentor training and filled out an application. I was interviewed by a CFES graduate, a mentor, and our school's liaison who asked questions about why I wanted to be a mentor and how I would handle certain situations. "

She continued, "I became a mentor to eight of my peers. I helped them with their academics. If teachers were having problems with my mentees, they would come to me and I would work with the students to help fix the problem. But my favorite lesson was teaching the students to advocate for themselves." It's a lesson Azeezat claims she learned early on and an important one to pass on.

"We went on college trips with our mentees," she added. "We are the leaders and everyone knows that we are CFES Scholars," she said.

During her senior year, Azeezat and her peers recommended that CFES become a full course.

"CFES is too important to be an after-school extracurricular," she said. "Our advisors agreed and it became part of our schedule. The extra time allowed us to make a road map for applying to college, create a resume, and look into internship opportunities."

Azeezat interned at JPMorgan Chase & Co. in 2015 and started at Barnard College that fall, studying pre-med courses.

"I'm a first generation college student and I didn't have any home guidance," she stated. "If it wasn't for CFES, I wouldn't have been invited to the White House."

Her advisor read four of Azeezat's personal statements before he told her that she had a good one, and according to her he "will tell you how it is." In doing so, he's looking out for his students, which is exactly what he did when he recommended Azeezat for the White House summit.

"There is a lot of data that will say you can't do it . . . but you can. You have to stay humble and focused," said the First Lady to a room full of eager students, going on to say, "If I had listened to people that said I couldn't do it, I wouldn't be here today."

The students in attendance participated in paying for college and other sessions, and during one of these panels, the President unexpectedly made an appearance.

"President Obama just popped in," Azeezat exclaimed. "I got to shake his hand. He was only there for 5 minutes, but his words will stay with me forever: 'Don't let anybody discourage you! You have to use education as a tool.'"

Building Pathways Knowledge

Early exposure to college pathways makes higher education seem less like a pipe dream and more a realistic possibility, as one school in Wilmington, DE, has shown (Box 5.9).

> ## Box 5.9 *Middle School Students Become College and Career Ready in Wilmington, Delaware*
>
> Learning about college begins in the 6th grade at Bayard Middle School, where CFES Scholars research different geographic areas from Hawaii to Florida to New England and compile information regarding the colleges in each particular area. In 7th grade, the research focuses on career options.
>
> Then in the 8th grade, Scholars focus on a college and a career of their choosing. This final step involves writing to the colleges to request information. Scholars were thrilled to get responses and even trinkets from colleges! Charel, an 8th-grade Scholar, was excited when the college she chose sent information and a letter addressed to her.
>
> Their research completed, each 8th grader created a trifold table-top display to share with their classmates, younger peers, and teachers. They also completed college applications. One Scholar's sister is in the 12th grade, and she pointed out that her sister "doesn't have the support that we do. When she complains about filling out college applications, I know it really is doable." In fact, "I've been helping my older sister fill out her applications."

After years of working in urban schools, CFES professionals have seen countless students benefit from developing the *Essential Skills*. A professor and team of doctoral students from the University of Michigan reinforced this anecdotal evidence by conducting focus groups and qualitative evaluation at four CFES schools in New York City and found through patterns of student engagement that Scholars are developing the *Essential Skills*.

Developing *Essential Skills*

By engaging in CFES core practices that build socio-cultural understanding of college pathways, students are empowered to overcome barriers in their communities and develop the *Essential Skills*—grit, leadership, teamwork, raised aspirations, perseverance, and adaptability. (While this section highlights examples from urban schools, the techniques are applicable to all audiences.)

Grit: Determination and Passion to Reach Long-term Goals

Scholars who plot a course for college and establish career pathways need to develop and draw on deep reservoirs of perseverance and confidence to realize their goals. They cannot do this on their own: The social support they receive through CFES activities enables them to build these traits (Box 5.10; the quotes in Box 5.10 are from focus groups in urban schools conducted by the University of Michigan researchers.)

Box 5.10 *Evidence of Grit**

Students Respond to Support

- "A couple of teachers saw my potential and they kept pushing. I wasn't in engineering and they kept pushing for me to join the program . . . You had to keep an 85 average. It was a way of them trying to get me to raise my standards. They kept pushing it on me. And I finally caved."

- "I know for me as a freshman, I was extremely shy . . . then sophomore year, I got involved in Band . . . I think the programs in the school, especially Leadership and CFES, have helped me to be more well-spoken—outspoken."

- "I heard about it my freshman year. I actually had (teacher) for my Life Skills class. So in the Life Skills class he said, 'You're a good student. You should [join] CFES.' So once I joined I went on college trips."

Students Learn to Navigate Systems

- ". . . when I realized that they [teacher and staff] came back and actually were attacking me saying, 'You have this potential you're

---

wasting.' It gave me a reality check . . . They changed my mindset and made me more interactive with CFES . . . that goes back to me like—wow, they see this potential and I didn't use it."

- "Freshman year, I thought I had school in the bag. Like, school and all the tests were easy. I got my first report card and I failed a class and had a 73 average . . . now, three years later, it is almost 85. Now I take school seriously because I saw the competition. It's hard out there."

- "'Why can't I push myself that much harder?' It depends on how much you really focus. If you give something then the results will show. My mother has told me that time after time."

* These quotes are from focus group interviews conducted in May 2013 by University of Michigan researchers.

Leadership: Problem Solving through Project-based Learning

CFES core practices provide Scholars with opportunities to tackle real-world challenges that concern them, such as bullying, gender inequalities, career awareness, hunger, and homelessness (Box 5.11). These activities, many of which are outside the classroom, support development of leadership skills.

Teamwork: Collaborate on Projects

Scholars learn about teamwork through activities and one-on-one problem solving. As students participate in Leadership Through Service projects, they learn to work with others. Mentoring also develops teamwork—not only do Scholars learn how to accept guidance from mentors, but the mentors learn how to support others (Box 5.12).

Box 5.11 *Evidence of Leadership*

Group Problem-Solving

- "All through our freshman year and sophomore year, everything has been told to us to do. Being a part of leadership, we can set up all these things. I felt like we can change things up a little bit so it'll be really cool."

- "We focus on the networking aspect. It really helps us to network and meet people, how to greet people. Those simple things you forget can cost you a job—can cost you a college acceptance . . . It's really helpful in the communication aspect and breaking out of our shells."

- "I thought that leadership would help me become the leader I want to be. Mentoring increased my passion for leadership. In college I definitely want to be a leader because I want to inspire people."

- "CFES was a chance for us to show that we were leaders. And through CFES we have the chance to show that and to prove to ourselves and other people that we could lead."

Box 5.12 *Evidence of Teamwork*

Leadership Through Service

- "My junior year I participated in the leadership summit at the Apollo (Harlem, NYC). I got to speak to the whole group of CFES students about my experience in CFES."

- "Different schools in the district came here for CFES. We were talking about politics, how we can involve more adolescents in politics. Different things, community service and all the different things we can involve adolescents in."

Raising Aspirations: Overcoming Family and Community Barriers to Higher Education Goals

Raising aspirations is a multifaceted process that involves communication with families about barriers and opportunities (Box 5.13). Students are able to build the knowledge for this process through school–college–community networks. Students build a realistic understanding of the financial barriers they face as they learn about college costs and financial aid. Financial awareness empowers them to overcome their fears about college costs, but also develop realistic plans for college.

Box 5.13 *Evidence of Raised Aspirations*

Making Good Choices

- "The main thing is I learned what to look for in a college . . . I picked my high school for a stupid reason. I was like—I don't want to wear a uniform for four years. Luckily, I landed in a pretty good school. I didn't want to pick a college for a stupid reason. CFES showed me this is what you should be looking for in a school—these are the standards you should be setting for yourself—and they gave me a roadmap."

- "I'm not coming from the greatest household, financial-wise. Also, I'm a role model for younger siblings and cousins. I want to be the stepping-stone that they use to be better than me and not to be on the same path. I want to set high standards so they can surpass me."

- "I would definitely say to join CFES. It gives you that motivation, networking skills, leadership skills and speaking skills as well. I think that without CFES I wouldn't be the person I am today. I'm focused. And it gives you that career-oriented thing—like training, I guess, in a way and the college experience overall. I think it's worth it."

Financial Realism

- "Before last year, I thought college would be more scary because you're going away. You don't know anyone at first. And then the work seems really hard. But after we visited I noticed you will learn how to manage your work. The one thing I was most scared about was financial aid. Even though there are scholarships, most colleges right now are really expensive and so that was my worry."

- "The first semester we started in CFES—they give out the FAFSA information . . . the common applications and how to answer them. Then we started doing our college essays. People come in to tutor us. And so we do everything."

- "Last year when I was a junior my main goal was just apply, apply, apply for scholarships, internships, so I can get some money and pay for my tuition and for my books. Don't lose the deadline. You want to beat the deadline."

Value of CFES

- "Not only do I really want to go to college, I know I can do well in college because I'm very determined. And that's because of CFES. When I went on those trips, I saw—if they can do it—why can't I? . . . The only concern I could possibly ever have is time management. And that's the concern most people have throughout their entire life. But it's just setting your priorities straight. I know I'm going to college to be a student full-time."

- "They have taught us to sell ourselves, give ourselves a three-minute introduction to someone . . . like an elevator speech. They taught us that and taught us how to present ourselves as a brand."

Perseverance: Toughness and Ego Strength to Help Students Achieve Long-term Goals

Having high aspirations along with a realistic understanding of college costs provides students with inner strength and awareness that helps them prepare for the hard work required to attain their college dreams and build understanding of the ways completing college is intertwined with their hope for career opportunities related to their interests and abilities (Box 5.14).

Box 5.14 *Evidence of Perseverance*

College Goals

- "My problem will most likely be the workload. I have a tendency to leave things for the last minute. Lately, I have been improving—actually putting in work—doing outlines and time management. Even though it's due next month or so—I need to get in the habit of actually doing things before time instead of waiting till the last minute."

- "It takes hard work. You can't expect to get into a college without working and taking time out to search and look and apply. It's time management and also hard work and putting your mind to it."

- "I saw that a [college] student, just like myself, was a freshman, and they were doing work like I was. It made my perception a whole lot different, a whole lot clearer. It made me feel better about college students. They're just like me."

Career Goals

- "I feel if I don't go to college, I'm not going to get a good job. My life is going to fail without college. Going to college is going to further my education and better my life as well. Because once I get to college and get that degree, I have a better chance of getting better jobs than a person with a high school diploma."

"I want to join the military but I'm still thinking about going to college as well. It was 50–50 at one point. But through CFES I noticed it is better to go through college and join ROTC. Right now, I'm looking at West Point. I have the requirements that they're looking for. I'm motivated to be able to apply there."

Adaptability: Flexibility when Working with People with Different Views and Cultures

CFES helps students learn that one's choice of career influences the college they pick—and, likewise, the college they pick can influence the career they enter. Scholars learn that adapting to diverse settings and people is integral to college success, as is learning about the nature of work through internships and exposure to work settings related to their career interests (Box 5.15).

Box 5.15 *Evidence of Adaptability*

College Planning

- "Social life at college is something I'm thinking about a lot because that's the place you are going to be for the next four years of your life . . . I want to go somewhere that's diverse, somewhere that fits my needs, someplace that I know is just for me . . . it doesn't have to be Harvard or some school like that. If the school fits me personally then that's the school I want to go for."

- "I wouldn't go to a school that's predominantly black or predominantly white. I'd like to go to a school that's mixed because when I'm out in the real world I'm not going to deal with just only Caucasians or African Americans. I'm going to deal with a broad range of individuals."

- "I believe that it's better to have a diverse group of friends . . . You can see things from other people's point of view rather than just seeing things from always one side."

Career Planning

- "I've been working with a doctor since junior year . . . it's more money . . . you're going to have a job forever. They're guiding me towards medical programs. I'm choosing . . . City [CUNY] because it has really good pre-optometry major."

Conclusion

The challenges facing urban low-income students are great and many urban educators feel the systemic constraints imposed by standards, aligned curriculum, and standardized tests as controlling mechanisms. These centrally controlled schemes of teacher accountability constrain opportunities for teachers to provide socio-cultural experiences that help level the playing field of college access and success. Yet providing opportunities for urban students to build their essential skills for college and career readiness is possible, especially when they work in partnerships with others in local networks. Narrowing the opportunity gap can be accelerated when students: learn about college and career pathways, engage in meaningful conversations with adults who have traveled these pathways, and build essential skills by working with peers in projects supporting their own communities.

Information alone is not the answer because students can experience false advertising that is consonant with real-life voices and experiences. School–college–community networks can provide the additional support necessary to empower students to take these steps. Involving student advocates in businesses, hospitals, churches, and other community-based organization is crucial. The core practices provide means for engaging the diverse members of urban communities in providing support that accelerates learning of skills essential to college a career success. Listening to what students say provides the evidence base for building local practices that empower students.

6 | Rural Schools

Box 6.1 *College and the Rural Challenge**

The rural school district of Ticonderoga, NY, has a lot going for it that other places may envy. Its halls are safe. Children in Ticonderoga are part of a small community that keeps an eye on them as they grow up.

But it is also being hammered by poverty.

Nearly one out of every two students in the town's school system qualifies for free or reduced-cost lunch. Just 20 years ago, that figure was 12 percent.

Ticonderoga, a town of 5,100 on the shores of Lake Champlain and Lake George, struggles every day with something more and more rural communities are forced to confront: a surging tide of poverty that threatens to keep its students from ever attaining a college education.

This tide is eroding what communities can expect from their children and lessening hope for their futures. Students are being kept from college not so much because they can't afford it, but because they can't imagine it.

And while we don't know how to fix poverty, we do know how to overcome its effects.

Over the last few years, a growing chorus has expressed concern about the rising costs of attending college and the threat this poses to accessibility.

For many rural children, though, tuition is just the final hurdle they face on the road to college. Drug use, dropping in cities, is increasing in rural areas around the country. Teen pregnancy and sexually transmitted diseases are also on the rise. The common denominator these rural areas share is poverty. Of the nation's 250 most impoverished counties, 244 are rural.

The key to developing rural communities is to prepare children for college and career. It all starts with education—and all of us must get started.

In Ticonderoga, and throughout neighboring schools in the Adirondacks, students and instructors from institutions including Plattsburgh State, Paul Smith's College and Middlebury College mentor students, coach them on service projects, make regular appearances in their schools and, perhaps most important, bring students as young as fourth grade to their campuses to expose them to worlds they have never seen before.

Today, it is almost impossible to break out of the poverty cycle without a college degree; jobs that pay well, difficult to find in rural America, depend on a degree.

Perversely, this is one of the very reasons we find that expectations for rural students are so low. In urban areas, families increasingly understand that sending a child to college gives that child a chance to move ahead. But rural families often feel threatened when their children want to go off to college—because when they go, they may be leaving for good. As a result, some families don't pass the dream along to their children, and the children don't pick it up on their own.**

* Dalton & Mills (2008).
** Beeson & Strange (2000).

Rural schools, like the ones in Ticonderoga, face different challenges than urban schools. Options for partnerships with corporations and nonprofits are limited because of long distances and small populations (Box 6.1). Rural families fear losing their children if they go to college. "Word spreads that college is a one-way ticket out of town, and for a lot of kids, that deflates their interest to go to school," says Tony Collins, president of Clarkson University in Potsdam, NY. "We have to reverse that mindset."[1]

Another challenge in some rural communities is second-home owners who may resist school taxes, often because they are already paying taxes in the communities where their children attend school. "Second-home owners are typically seen as part of the problem," Collins said. Willsboro Central School superintendent, Steve Broadwell, tackled this issue through a community-based mentoring program described later in this chapter.

This chapter describes barriers facing rural educators and shares innovative strategies to meet these challenges. CFES has a unique perspective on serving rural populations because its roots are in rural schools (Chapter 1); its headquarters are located in a community of just 600 full-time residents. CFES is one of very few global nonprofits that provide college and career readiness support to both urban and rural communities. To this day, rural issues remain at the core of CFES's efforts: it pledges that at least a third of the schools it works with will be in rural communities.

Organizing in Rural Communities and Schools

Peak Experiences, a book about raising the aspirations and educational achievement of rural youth in the Adirondacks of New York State, describes the unique challenges faced by rural schools.[2]

- The impact of economic change has been dire for rural America. Local economies have suffered as jobs in agriculture, mining, logging and other industries have weakened or died out. Jobs have been lost, stores shuttered. Family incomes have diminished.

- The *Encyclopedia of Rural America* noted that "the employment picture rural youth face after high school is bleak because today's economy is an urban economy." The Encyclopedia notes "low-skill, low-paying jobs remain in the countryside, whereas high-paying jobs are in the cities to which rural America's most talented youth are drawn."[3]

- Despite this, rural communities and schools are critical to our nation. Defining rural as communities of fewer than 2,500 residents, 30 percent of all public schools are in rural areas along with nearly 20 percent of the nation's public school students—almost 9 million in total attend rural schools.[4]

To analyze rural communities and schools and the impact of CFES in them, graduate students from the University of Michigan conducted interviews with CFES Scholars, educators and volunteers in five rural school districts in New York and Florida. Interviewers asked participants about their experiences with the core practices: Pathways, Leadership Through Service, and Mentoring.

Socio-Cultural Support for Academic Capital Formation

CFES core practices and the social processes related to ACF (described in Chapter 3) are closely related. Each core practice overlapped with ACF processes, with the exception of family uplift. Three other factors identified as central to program success in these schools—Capacity for Change (C), Selection Process (S), and Financial Aid (FA) —are listed in the column on school contexts (Table 6.1).

Each of these five rural schools developed a *capacity for change* (C) and became exemplary schools. The social support provided by CFES was

Table 6.1 Alignment of CFES Core Practices and the Social Cultural Support with Consideration of School Capacity and Student Selection*

CFES Core Practices/ Academic Capital Formation	School Contexts • Capacity (C) • Selection (S) • Financial Aid (FA)	Pathways	Mentoring	Leadership
Concern about Costs	S, C, FA	X	X	X
Supportive Networks	C	X	X	X
Trustworthy Information	S, C	X	X	X
College Knowledge		X	X	X

Key: X denotes overlap

Note: * This table was previously published by Dalton, Bigelow, & St. John (2012).

a crucial factor, as the schools developed the core practices that eased concerns about costs, helped build supportive networks, and provided trustworthy information. Since the schools are focused on content knowledge, the formation of college knowledge and family uplift occurs within families and communities, but can also be aided by the core practices provided by school–college–community networks.

Concerns about Costs

Researchers found that information about college costs and aid helped students set a course toward college and empowered families to deal with their financial concerns. In particular, scholarships motivate students (Box 6.2).

Box 6.2 *Community Scholarships Boost College Readiness*

In 2006, CFES Program Director Carol Cathey shared with Ticonderoga, NY educators the story of a program created in her hometown in Florida, the Port St. Joe Scholarship Program, which has helped several hundred youth pay for college over the past two decades.

The story Cathey told launched the Ticonderoga Alumni Association, which sought to unify its graduates in order to raise the aspirations of rural students and move them toward college success. Since then, Ticonderoga has raised $150,000 and supported 397 students on the path to college.

All Ticonderoga students who pursue college are eligible for the scholarship. Amounts are determined by a formula that considers non-academic factors, including attendance, parental participation at school events (such as family workshops on paying for college), and school engagement. "It shows our students that there are many factors to success, not only good grades, and shows them that their school and community are committed to helping them succeed after high school," said Ticonderoga superintendent John McDonald.

Organizational Capacity for Change

A rural school superintendent described his goal "of going from good to great." His vision was to create a climate that embraced new methods and engaged students in building college knowledge. He knew that embedding CFES in the school curriculum meant building the capacity for change. Milford Central School (Chapter 3) did this when they embedded CFES by creating two dedicated CFES courses. Several other CFES schools now offer classes that include lessons on leadership development, steps toward college readiness, and building the *Essential Skills.* The principal at St. Joseph's Rush in Ireland, as described in Chapter 7, "adopted a whole school approach to implementing the practices. Every student in the school became involved with CFES and, as a result, every student became a CFES Scholar. This was done to encourage a greater cultural shift across the staff and student body and would echo other embedded inclusive practices within the school."

Administrators, students, and teachers in the New York and Florida rural schools noted that squeezing in college visits is challenging, as was evident in interviews.[5] Visits to college campuses often take a full day for students from schools in rural areas, as distances can be great. The resulting absences often throw off class plans in core courses. In mathematics, for example, a huge amount of predetermined content rests on standardized tests. Traveling to a college may mean missing a critical math test or a class session covering content necessary for these assessments.

CFES board member Dreama Gentry, Executive Director in Education Programs at Berea College in Kentucky, grew up in a rural community in the Appalachian Mountains. She's all too familiar with the challenges students from out-of-the-way communities face in getting ready for college. Despite obstacles, she says students with the ambition to achieve can find ways to do so (Resource 6.1).

"When I came to college," Gentry said, "I found my campus was very similar to the small town where I grew up. The skills that I developed growing up in rural America helped me find my place. The campus community became my support network, much like my family and small town had been my support system back home."[6]

Because rural schools are so small, some institutions involve all students in the CFES program rather than a select group. A student at an

Resource 6.1 *Strategies for College Readiness**

- Your school may have limited rigorous courses, such as Advanced Placement courses. Talk to your guidance counselor and do some research. Many state departments of education and community colleges offer online AP courses or first-year college courses. Guidance counselors can often find funds to cover the fees for these courses if you ask.

- The closest college or university may be hours away. I was a junior in high school before I ever visited a college campus. See if there are college access programs like Upward Bound and GEAR UP that serve your school. These programs can help you prepare for college and provide you with opportunities to visit college campuses.

- The Internet opens a world of possibilities to students from rural America. If you cannot visit a campus, participate in online campus tours. You can experience the campus, hear from current students, and get a feel for what the campus is like.

- Many rural areas lack diversity. Seek out opportunities to meet and interact with people from different backgrounds and cultures. Talk with your family about hosting an international student, or participate in clubs and organizations that provide opportunities to interact with diverse groups of people.

* Gentry (2015)

institution with a schoolwide CFES program said, "We have 20-something students in each grade. I've learned that people do believe in you and that you can do it."

In this case, peer pressure had a positive influence on CFES participation. There are other ways, too, in which self-selection and motivation spur involvement. For example, family engagement in college site visits motivates planning for enrollment in both four-year colleges *and* technical programs.

CFES developed projects in rural Gulf County, Florida. One community there, Port St. Joe (Box 6.2), had a minority graduation rate that ranked 38th in the state in 2003–04. Four years later, it ranked No. 1 in Florida; by the 2008–09 academic year, the graduation rate for African American students in Gulf County schools was 95.7 percent.[7] Engaging students in CFES practices expanded opportunities not only for African American youth, but for their white peers in this rural community.

As another example, when CFES first began working with Crown Point Central School, a rural district in New York State's Adirondack region, the high school graduation and college-going rates were 54 and 43 percent respectively; eight years later, both rates exceeded 90 percent.

Mentoring empowers students to develop navigational skills that help them select and apply to college and for financial aid. College visits, mentoring by college students, and developing service projects all play substantial roles in changing students' orientation toward college. Perhaps most important, bullying behavior nearly disappeared in CFES rural schools. Strong and supportive cultures developed in all of these schools as part of their socio-cultural changes.[8]

One example of successful mentoring by community members in a rural school began in 2010 in Willsboro, NY. When Superintendent Steve Broadwell learned about EY's College Mentoring for Access and Persistence (MAP) program (Chapter 1), he asked CFES, "Why can't we set up the same model here?" Though the EY program is exclusively for urban communities, Broadwell and CFES went on to create a program in which 45 community members—about half of whom had once been second-home owners in Willsboro but had moved to the community full time—began mentoring every 11th and 12th grader in the school. John (Box 6.3) was one of those mentees.

Engagement: Gateways Opened in Rural Communities

CFES Scholars in rural communities are often a long distance from colleges and businesses that provide 21st-century jobs. Their involvement with CFES affords them opportunities to connect with other CFES Scholars and colleges outside their local communities, participate in virtual CFES workshops, and discussions with college and career professionals. "My students have

Box 6.3 *Creating a College Culture Nationwide: Big Vision in a Small Town**

You're a 16-year-old high school student scraping by with a C average. Your parents never went to college and it's the last thing on the minds of the kids you spend most of your time with. But then you decide to pursue a degree—and figure out how to raise your GPA, find financial aid, and get accepted to the institution that's just right for you.

If you're a low-income student from rural America, that story is a dream. Only 27 percent of 18- to 24-year-olds from rural areas enroll in higher education; nationally, only 11 percent of students from the families in the bottom economic quartile graduate from four-year colleges.

Five years ago, John, who lived in Willsboro, NY, was a mediocre student who hadn't even considered higher education. When a teacher encouraged him to buckle down academically and think about college, he faced ridicule from peers who told him it was a waste of time. Fortunately, a mentor convinced him to press on, urging him every day to study. He received weekly reminders to sign up for the ACT and SAT and extensive hands-on help in finding financial aid.

Today, John is a college junior with a 3.62 GPA. He's proud of what he has accomplished, but he also knows he didn't achieve success on his own. "There's no way I could have done this without lots of help from other people," he says. "My mentor pushed and pushed me to do better—to stop settling for average and raise my own standards."

John was lucky. The guidance he received didn't just show him the way to college—it also helped him realize the important role he could play in helping others find their way, too. Through service activities to improve his school and community, participation at a national conference and constant encouragement, John found that he had as much responsibility for helping others as others felt to help him. That sense of becoming part of a community—not just a charity recipient—is integral to CFES's strategy.

A few months into his college journey, John reached back to two longtime friends who had dropped out of college and convinced them to give it another try. His "if I can do it, you can too" attitude paid big dividends. Today they room together at SUNY Canton. They all have GPAs above 3.6. They're all on track to graduate and enter the 21st-century workforce. And together they offer a great example of what can happen when aspirations are instilled and fulfilled.

* Dalton (2013).

established a virtual partnership with an Irish CFES school," said Crystal Farrell, a teacher in Crown Point, NY. "An additional benefit of this partnership has been educators connecting to a global network."

Through their engagement in the core practices, students learn about new opportunities, as illustrated by responses to the CFES-administered surveys.

Pathways

CFES involvement yielded similar results among students in urban and rural schools, though Scholars in the rural schools had slightly fewer opportunities to visit college campuses and to talk with college students (Table 6.2) than did other CFES students. This difference is largely an artifact of the distance between the schools and college partners. In contrast, a slightly higher percentage of rural students reported they knew the courses they needed for college, probably because small schools have limited course offerings.

Mentoring and Social Support

While the five schools visited by the University of Michigan team had evidence of strong mentoring practices, rural Scholars were less likely to have adult mentors, likely because of distance to businesses and colleges (Table 6.3).

Table 6.2 Rural Scholars' Engagement in College/Career Pathways Practices

	Rural CFES Schools %	All CFES %
CFES scholar (self-identify)	95	93
Talked to college student last year	58	71
College students visited my school last year	61	63
College representative visited last year	58	55
Visited college campus last year	67	79
I know about financial aid/scholarships	91	91
I know the courses I need for college	78	72
I talk with my family about college	80	81
Need to improve grades for best college	91	92

Table 6.3 Rural Scholars' Engagement in Mentoring and Social Support

	Rural CFES Schools %	All CFES %
I know college dropouts	62	51
Talked with older student about problems	41	38
Older student is a mentor	24	42
Adult mentor (teacher, counselor, other)	57	63
Mentor makes it easy to ask questions	62	72
Teachers encourage college plans	89	88
Mentor encourages me to think about college	65	74
I am a mentor	40	45

Similar to the respondent population as a whole, most rural Scholars were involved in service through their schools, engaged in out-of-class projects, and worked on problem solving with other students. These activities were not only part of the leadership core practice, they also empowered students to build *Essential Skills*.

Essential Skills

The isolation of rural schools makes it difficult to provide opportunities beyond basic, day-to-day education. While traditional student activities like sports and music are pervasive, rural institutions often find it more challenging to launch more innovative programs. They have more difficulty establishing school–college–community networks than schools in urban and suburban communities, for example, simply because they're remote. CFES has developed school and college partnerships as well as virtual networks and resources to help bridge this gap. These strategies have helped students gain exposure to college and build the *Essential Skills*.

Grit: Determination and Passion for Long-term Goals

One benefit of engaging students in reflective conversations about college is that they build an understanding of what it takes to graduate, as demonstrated by an exchange in a focus group about college dropouts. According to one student, "a lot of the kids that have been active members in CFES have stayed in school, and they're still in college." Beyond merely observing dropouts, Scholars were aware that their peers who had engaged in CFES developed the grit to stay in college and the mettle to succeed. One middle school student described how she embraced grit in her life after a workshop "I'm going to be gritty, which means trying my best, not giving up, and trying again until I get it correct. Doing this is going to help my future."

Leadership: Problem Solving through Project-based Learning

In addition to participating in CFES leadership activities (Chapter 5), Scholars attended regional summits and national conferences that helped them develop social and leadership skills. For example, one student described how a leadership workshop helped him learn he had "the capability to lead anything. It's inspired me to take responsibility and achieve great things." Strategies for organizing leadership workshops are available through CFES (Resource 6.2).

126

Resource 6.2 *CFES Student Leadership Summits*

One of the most successful CFES Leadership Through Service activities is the Student Leadership Summit, a leadership development opportunity that maximizes student engagement and networking, and builds and strengthens student leadership skills.

During these workshops, which are planned and facilitated by CFES Scholars, participants address leadership topics and skill areas, share their leadership experiences, and brainstorm Leadership Through Service activities designed to make their schools and communities better places. Topics focus on early college awareness, goal setting, leadership development, peer mentoring, healthy habits, and social responsibility. The summit traditionally features a welcome and/or keynote speaker, breakout sessions to encourage discussion, and a closing session to share group findings and next steps.

A sample agenda:

9:30 am	Welcome, Introductions and Event Overview
9:50–10:50 am	Group Discussions (Sample Topics):
	Leading with Accountability and Responsibility
	Community Building and Empowerment 101
	The Leader's Identity: Who Are You?
	Communication Etiquette
11:00–12:00 pm	Group Discussions (Sample Topics):
	Leadership Beyond the Position
	Communicating Effectively
	Understanding the Value of Teamwork
	College and Careers: Where Are You Headed?
12:00–12:45 pm	Reporting Out, Lunch and Closing Remarks
1:00 pm	**Adjourn**

Teamwork: Collaboration on Projects Involving Communication and Problem Solving

Learning to collaborate involves more than getting into groups to do projects, a regular practice in many schools. As illustrated by a focus group conversation about communication skills learned at leadership conferences, Scholars reflect on how their experiences informed their interactions in their school (Box 6.4). This illustrates basic ways that CFES support builds a culture that supports teamwork, a skill colleges look for and most occupations require.

Raised Aspirations: Overcoming Family and Community Barriers to Setting Higher Education Goals

In communities with high poverty, students are expected to contribute to their families, including financially. One student commented, "I just want

Box 6.4 *Focus Group Reflections on Learning to Collaborate*

- "Just . . . interacting with the other kids from different schools, you know, like joking around, talking . . . that's probably the best part of the field trip."

- "At first, the trips, going on trips, you know, we get to have fun, whatever. But then you get used to you, um, you just like, get into the conversation and stuff . . . You just want to learn about it and stuff. And they then help you out . . . You just help out in the school. So you come back here and do better and stuff, so it was pretty neat . . . [to] be able to do stuff like that."

- "Yeah, it's more than a friendship: everyone is just nice to each other."

- "Before . . . there was a lot of like, cliques and stuff, but now everyone's just friends with everyone . . . There is some people that don't like each other, but that is . . . a problem in every school."

to get a full scholarship because these are hard times. My mom has given up a lot for us." This student saw her path to college as a continuum. "She's [her mother] been in a college, but . . . she had me. She decided to give it all up . . . I want to . . . give her money and let her do whatever she wants because she's already done enough." Most of the educators recognized that their students had family obligations and ties.

The Pathways to College and Career core practice builds students' navigational skills so they can work through the social and cultural barriers to college success. This practice overcomes the limitations of the narrower conception of academic preparation for college as content in required courses. An example: A mentor in upstate New York commented: "CFES has been wonderful for that [filling in the gaps for families with no history of college], because parents don't know how to even get started or to support them. In fact, a lot of times they'll say, 'I can't, my parents say there's not money.' And we have to kind of break through that and work with the families."

When Scholars decide to engage in CFES, they're exposed to support activities that help them overcome barriers to college. These activities, such as workshops and college visits, help raise aspirations in spite of social pressures in their own families and communities that hinder pursuit of higher education, as illustrated by students' reflections on how their engagement helped them raise their aspirations (Box 6.5).

Perseverance: Toughness and Ego Strength Helps Students Achieve Long-term Goals

Many activities constructed through the core practices provide students with opportunities to actualize long-term goals and overcome social and financial barriers. Just gaining information on student financial aid, for example, is enough to convince many students that there are avenues open to them to pay for college (Box 6.6). Students who gain a realistic understanding of financial barriers and strategies to surmount them, such as identifying scholarships and grants and learning to write aid applications, are empowered to engage in family conversations about college opportunities. This knowledge helps students and families to cope with concerns about costs.

Box 6.5 *Raised Aspirations through Engagement in CFES*

- "It's opened our eyes to what's out there. And made us want to go to college because it can lead us to a better place and everything."

- "I wasn't sure I was about going to college. But when I got in CFES, I started thinking about it and when I got going to different colleges ... It was seeing ... different classes ... and different options you have, and that's what made me want to go."

- "I found out about, you know, how good it is ... It introduces you to the college aspect ... something that a lot of people really don't think about. And one good thing: they drill into you about the whole college thing ..."

- "At first, I really didn't care about school ... and then, in this program, it just helped me a lot and made me realize I do want to go to college ..."

Box 6.6 *Learning about Financial Aid Builds Strength to Persevere*

- "I think that they should talk to us more about financial aid because I didn't know what I was getting into."

- "Before I got into the program, I was just hoping somebody would tell me about a scholarship, or hoping that a school would contact me. But being in the program, it gives me that little bit of know-how."

- "I didn't realize how important it was [to apply for aid] until I talked to the schools. They told me I needed to fill out my FAFSA if I wanted to get money. So, I [have] mine done."

- "My mom always asked me how much money it costs to be in college."

Conclusion

The more remote nature of rural areas makes it as difficult for professional educators to keep up with national trends and best practices as it is for students to have meaningful interactions with adult mentors and visit college campuses. Districts that participate in CFES, though, are able to tap into a national network that helps fill a void created by shrinking staffs in high schools and wide geography. While many districts have just one teacher per subject area and one counselor per school, the challenges they face—Common Core standards, Advanced Placement classes, and other academic topics—are shared among all of them. The CFES National Conference and other gatherings create time and space for educators to discuss best practices in a supportive, forward-thinking environment.

Other programs, such as a fellowship program connecting high school teachers with college professors, and rural–urban exchanges of Scholars and teachers are critical to making out-of-the-way schools more in the mainstream.

Taking Action

The Irish Case

Cliona Hannon and Katriona O'Sullivan

After scanning the globe to find a proven method for encouraging college and career readiness, Cliona Hannon contacted Rick Dalton about the possibility of using the CFES model in Ireland, starting in schools servicing low-income schools in Dublin. By adding the local networks using the core practices to the array of programs, Trinity has expanded college opportunities for students formerly excluded because of deep cultural barriers. The Trinity Access Programmes (TAP) have developed their own distinctive approach to create new avenues into colleges and career access and we encourage schools, colleges, and communities to adopt and adapt these coherent and cohesive practices.

TAP is now organizing student advocates in communities across Ireland into local partnerships that empower low-income students to bust those old class barriers that constrained their college access. In the "Irish Case" that follows, Cliona Hannon and Katriona O'Sullivan explain how they have seized the opportunity to adapt the CFES model to meeting the needs of schools, educators, and students as they bust through the chains of social. They use research to document the remarkable success of their pilot program. Irish eyes are smiling, indeed! The Irish story illustrates how social activists and student advocates can build networks that use the core practices to promote socially just, educational change. This story has global implications.

The Irish Case

In the early 1990s, Trinity College Dublin, the University of Dublin, Ireland, began to develop programs aimed at addressing the information gap for students in schools located in low-income communities. Established in 1592, Trinity is one of seven universities in the Republic of Ireland, and it is regarded as the most selective of the Irish higher education institutions. Through the Trinity Access Programmes (TAP), Trinity has developed a range of outreach activities, university foundation courses, and other alternative admissions routes that have enabled the progression of over 1,900 students from low-income backgrounds into the university since the early 2000s.

One Trinity College graduate who entered via the Trinity Access Programmes said: "Where I come from, no one went to college. Most of my friends and family ended up on social welfare or in prison. I had a baby young and while I knew I was bright, I never thought I would amount to anything. TAP gave me a space to believe in myself, it provided me with new role models and mentors I could relate to, and gave me the skills to be able to put my hand up and ask a question and not feel like I was going to be kicked out of the lecture theatre. College has changed my life; it has changed my whole family's lives."

TAP has inspired hundreds of stories like these, but hundreds are not enough: TAP administrators recognized that in order to achieve the reach they had in mind, they needed to serve more young people at an early enough stage in their educational development to have a significant impact on their life trajectory. When Rick Dalton, President and CEO of College For Every Student, met with Cliona Hannon, TAP's director, in 2011, they saw potential for collaboration. While the challenges were similar in the United States and Ireland—limited educational guidance, a dearth of professional role models, and school cultures where both teachers and students struggled to break a cycle of educational disadvantage—there were also differences in culture and context, which meant that materials drawn from one context would require thoughtful adaptation. Both organizations had to secure resources to facilitate the project pilot. This is where the partnership with College For Every Student began.

The Trinity College Dublin—CFES Partnership

TAP worked with one Irish school, St. Joseph's Secondary School in Rush, County Dublin, in 2013 to adapt CFES materials for the Irish market. Educators from Trinity College Dublin and St. Joseph's reworked those resources so the language and focus were more applicable for use in the

Irish educational system. These materials were tested with students and a wider group of educators before use. In addition, Irish educational experts developed resources to address issues like college financing and mentoring. In order to find mentors who fit in with the community and to whom students could relate, TAP recruited St. Joseph's alumni who had recently become students at Trinity or other higher education institutions.

It was clear from the results of the pilot project that the CFES model had potential to address Irish educational challenges. On the strength of that test run, Trinity secured support from Google for a three-year project known as Trinity Access 21-College For Every Student (TA21–CFES). Starting with 11 schools in low-income areas across Dublin, the longitudinal action-research project informed the development of the program as it unfolded. In the case of this project, each year the schools and the TA21 team use the research from the previous year to help shape what CFES will look like for the coming year. In 2014–15, 1,100 second-year students (age 14) completed the first year of this three-year program. The TA21–CFES program employs the three core practices of CFES (Mentoring, Leadership Through Service, and Pathways to College and Career), and will add a fourth practice focusing on 21st-century Teaching and Learning.

To establish evidence on the impact of the TA21–CFES project, the Irish program was designed in a more prescriptive way than the U.S. versions. Schools were asked to focus on all students in second year (age 14) over a three-year period, rather than a selection of second-year students. Schools were free, however, to involve additional students in the program.

The Irish Context

The Irish education system is broken down into three separate systems: primary (age 5–12), secondary (age 13–18), and third level (further and higher education). Higher education in Ireland results in a college or university degree; further education typically involves one or two years of vocational training, but can be used as a stepping stone to college. Before students pass out of secondary education, they are required to take an exam for what is known as a Leaving Certificate; their entrance into further and higher education is based on the points they earn on that test.

Most students enter their post-secondary courses in Ireland on the basis of these academic outcomes alone. Except for students with disabilities or from low-income backgrounds, other factors are not taken into consideration.[1] Entry requirements for any higher education course are determined by demand, so the most competitive (courses like pharmacy, law, or medicine) have the highest entry points requirement. Medicine in Trinity College Dublin, for example, usually has a points requirement of about 580 out of a maximum of 625 points, or the equivalent of four A grades and two B grades.

A member of the European Union, Ireland has set a goal of 72 percent of its students pursuing college degrees.[2] Some 54 percent of Irish young adults (18–20 year olds) now progress to higher education, and their degree completion rate averages 85 percent.[3]

While many of these efforts have proven effective, a recent report commissioned by Ireland's Higher Education Authority said the overall effect of these access initiatives had been dampened by entrenched social issues. "As a society we can acknowledge and celebrate the enormous strides in broadening access to higher education . . . But an uncomfortable and sobering fact is that deep reservoirs of educational disadvantage, mirroring in large part economic disadvantage, are also part of the Irish higher education story."[4] The report indicated that students in low-income areas are significantly less likely to have professional role models, career-focused guidance counseling, a culture of high expectations, and an active learning

• **Age 13** • **11 Subjects**
• **Age 14** • **11 Subjects**
• **Age 15** • **STATE EXAM: Junior Certificate**
• **Age 16** • **Transition Year (Flexible Curriculum)**
• **Age 16/17** • **7 Subjects**
• **Age 17/18** • **STATE EXAM: Leaving Certificate**

Figure 7.1 Primary and Secondary Levels in Ireland

environment whereby they are engaged in self-directed collaborative work practices, all of which support the development of college-going expectations.

"We spend more time dealing with students' personal issues than looking at their academic potential and planning for their future," said a project leader at one TA21–CFES school. "It is more like pastoral care than career guidance at times, with over 70 percent of our students having significant personal issues that stop them engaging in their education."

Low-income students in other developed countries face similar challenges. While overall numbers progressing to higher education have increased substantially in these countries since the 1980s, the progression rate of those students whose families live on the economic margins has been slow to shift. Research and practice both point to the importance of providing early, accurate information on progression options, offering a range of professional role models and opportunities to expand students' frames of reference, and imparting a sense that they have a voice in the educational process. Students are capable of setting high goals and working to achieve them. The TA21–CFES partnership aims to address these issues through a scaffolded approach using the CFES core practices of Mentoring, Leadership Through Service, and Pathways, along with the 21st century skills. The aim is to strengthen the capacity of the school so that the culture becomes one of high expectations, with students, teachers, and leadership all headed in the same direction.

Academic Capital Formation (ACF) Among Irish Students

The emergent theory of Academic Capital Formation (Chapter 2) provided a framework under which the CFES model was adapted to meet the needs of Irish students. CFES in Ireland did not initially focus as much on concerns about costs because higher education remains mainly publicly funded. Low-income students across Ireland can qualify for need-based grants that cover the full cost of college tuition as well as a small stipend.[5] It turned out, however, that many Irish students were unaware of the financial support available to them and not as well versed in their understanding of costs as we expected. Thus, we found there were concerns about cost among low-income students who actually had financial access.

In Ireland, as other places, low-income students are more likely to pursue higher education when they have access to networks that can help them understand the process.

- College students from TA21–CFES communities were recruited to serve as mentors. Most of these mentors had entered Trinity College via TAP.

- Low-income Irish students are often reluctant to commit to an educational path that does not have a defined career outcome.[6] To address some of these concerns, the TA21–CFES program includes information about career choices.

Table 7.1 identifies the main constructs of the TA21–CFES model, their relevance to low-income students, and how the model is addressing them.

Student Engagement in CFES Practices

The TA21–CFES project has already had a clear impact on both students' and teachers' visions for themselves and for each other. Early results show that students have higher professional aspirations and are demonstrating more awareness of their own potential. There is also a clear change in the classroom relationships, with students seeing their teachers as more accessible and supportive. Teachers and school leaders directly involved with the project have noted that the CFES model has had a pervasive impact across their institutions.

The Study of CFES Scholars

In the United States, the typical CFES school targets a minimum of 100 low-income students to participate in the program. In Ireland, the 11 schools participating in the TA21–CFES project are focusing on all students between the ages of 14–17 in order to develop sufficient data to support the program.

Each participating Irish school has incorporated TA21–CFES practices into the curriculum. Second-year students took surveys to measure their engagement with the core practices and the program's effect on college-going aspirations. Students also participated in interviews and focus groups.

Table 7.1 ACF Constructs and their Impact on Irish Low-income Students*

ACF Constructs	Challenges for Irish Low-Income Families	Core practice
Concerns about Costs	For low-income families, perceived and actual costs of higher education can be a barrier to access and progression.	1. Pathways 2. Mentoring
Supportive Networks	Low-income students are often influenced by community norms which may be more focused on employment than higher education. This may reduce the likelihood that information about how to navigate higher education will be transmitted.	1. Mentoring
Trusted Information	Information forms the basis for action. Low-income students often lack access to information that would support the likelihood of their progression to higher education. This includes information on courses, entry routes and requirements, and the availability of extra tuition courses to boost their final examination grades.	1. Mentoring 2. Pathways
College Knowledge	Low-income students lack basic knowledge about higher education, including entry requirements, financing, and the application process.	1. Pathways
Cultural Capital	This represents family knowledge of education, which may include positive and negative experiences. In high-progression families, cultural capital provides a resource that supports educational attainment across generations; this may be reversed in low-income families, which have a limited or negative educational history.	1. Pathways
Concerns about Career	Low-income students and their families may not understand the career paths associated with college degrees. This increases fear and reduces the likelihood they will participate.	1. Mentoring 2. Pathways 3. Leadership

* Table adapted from St. John et al. (2010, p. 43).

TA21–CFES Scholars: We compared the responses of 1,010 TA21–CFES Scholars with 238 students from non-CFES schools in both affluent and disadvantaged communities in Ireland. Students from affluent communities generally have high rates of transfer to university—70 percent, in this case—and are referred to as the "high control" group. We also included 196 students from schools located in low-income communities with low transfer rates to university (referred to as "low control"); their average transfer rate to university, 30 percent, matched that of the overall TA21 cohort. Comparing results of high- and low-control schools helps us understand the kind of changes that occur in the knowledge and confidence base of this age cohort when no organized college-going project such as TA21–CFES is present. Data were collected at the start of year one (this is baseline data) and at the end of year one. We discuss the student changes evident from the data as well as compare the TA21–CFES Scholars with the U.S. Scholars, to identify similarities and differences across the two jurisdictions.

Consistent with national research, the percentage of TA21–CFES Scholars reporting a family member with a four-year degree was lower than the high-control group. Interestingly, a significant proportion of students in all three groups did not know what level of education their parents had attained (Table 7.2).

Table 7.2 Highest Educational Attainment in TA21–CFES Ireland Scholar Families Compared with Overall U.S. CFES Cohort and Control Groups

	TA21-CFES Ireland %	All U.S. CFES %	High Control %	Matched Control %
Did not finish high school	10	6	2	15
High school diploma or GED or Leaving Certificate	18	16	12	20
Some college	16	25	14	10
Four-year degree or higher	14	31	49	9
Don't know	43	23	23	47

Pathways to College and Careers

For many students, even contemplating college seems a step too far—which is one reason why actually visiting a campus is such a critical part of the CFES experience. In focus groups and interviews, Scholars said that visiting university campuses broke some of the stereotypical ideas they had about higher education. Table 7.1 shows how university activities can have an important impact upon Scholars perceptions' of themselves and their potential. For some, it has given them more choice and broadened their frame of reference.

As part of the Pathways component, TA21–CFES Scholars visited college campuses, met college students, and completed a college investigation assignment that required them to analyze two courses (one with a STEM focus) and discuss collegiate entry requirements and career prospects with their families.

These practices paid off instantly. Through just one year of the project, Scholars in Ireland showed they were more immersed in some practices than the CFES students in the U.S. (Table 7.3); for example, 84 percent of TA21–CFES students spoke with a college student, compared to 71 percent of the U.S. students. The TA21–CFES students were more limited in their understanding than their American counterparts in two areas: recognition that their grades need to be improved in order to attend college; and knowledge of financial aid, likely because aid is a much more important component of the American college experience.

The number of TA21–CFES students planning to pursue a trade when they leave school decreased by 15 percent, while the number of students planning to progress to further education in a one–two year course increased by 10 percent and those planning on going on to university increased by 10 percent. Table 7.4 shows that the TA21–CFES and U.S. CFES Scholars have higher intentions to progress to further education than the low control group.

While more than half of the TA21–CFES Scholars indicated a plan to go to university, cost concerns may pose a significant barrier. Many students did not have a real understanding of university costs and often overestimated them. This was clear from student remarks made in the focus groups, in which Scholars expressed concern about the costs of higher education. Some said their families did not have enough money.[7] Even within individual schools, student knowledge of college costs varied (Box 7.1). This shows

Table 7.3 Engagement in College/Career Pathways Practices of TA21–CFES Students from Before and After Year One, Compared with Other Student Groups at End of 2014–2015 Academic Year

	Before Year One TA21–CFES %	After Year One TA21–CFES %	All U.S. CFES %	High Control %	Low Control %
Talked to college student last year	65	84	71	78	68
College students visited my school last year	46	83	63	27	51
Visited college campus last year	38	75	79	31	29
I know about financial aid/scholarships	41	57	91	56	58
I talk with my family about college	66	78	81	53	61
Need to improve grades for best college	62	64	92	37	58

that the initial presumption that Irish students did not need information about costs was incorrect. This was addressed through the introduction of a Pathways activity that informs students about grants and college tuition fees.

Engagement in TA21–CFES Mentoring and Social Support

Mentoring provides Scholars with attainable role models—people who are relatable and trustworthy. TA21–CFES Scholars participated in six structured mentoring sessions with a university student/graduate from their own community (Table 7.5).[8] Mentoring sessions, held in person or online,

Table 7.4 Plans After Completing School: CFES Scholars and Comparison Groups

	Before Year One TA21–CFES %	After Year One TA21–CFES %	All U.S. CFES %	High Control %	Low Control %
Work	12	10	6	5	17
One–two Year Further Education Course	50	60	7	42	53
Trade	49	34	2	29	44
University	50	60	65	50	56

* Columns add to more than 100 percent because in the survey for the TA-21 Scholars and the high and low control groups students were allowed to select more than one answer; the U.S. group could only select one.

Box 7.1 *TA21–CFES Scholars Lack Specific Knowledge of College Costs*

Interviewer: How much do you think it costs to go to college?

Student 1: It's like 5,000 (euro) or something.

Student 2: I don't know.

Student 3: 2,000.

Student 4: 8,000.

Student 5: It depends on what college you go to.

Student 6: I'm not sure I'm going to college because I have no money.

focused on time management and organization—topics adapted from versions of CFES's U.S. resources. For example, in the first year, mentors and mentees completed several worksheets and discussions focused on planning and study. At Mercy Secondary School, TA21–CFES Project Leader and Guidance Counselor Michelle O'Kelly shared her experience as a former

Table 7.5 Engagement in Mentoring and Social Support: TA21–CFES Scholars and Comparison Students

	Before Year One TA21–CFES %	After Year One TA21–CFES %	All U.S. CFES %	High Control %	Low Control %
I know college dropouts	42	39	51	30	42
Talked with older student about problems	37	36	38	23	37
Older student is a mentor	17	51	42	30	17
Adult mentor	37	56	63	22	37
My mentor encourages college plans	12	75	72	22	58
I have taken part in school mentoring program	10	77	100	28	10

pupil of the school and a member of the local community in order to support the students' educational aspirations. In Box 7.2 Michelle writes about the impact of TA21–CFES in the school, and in Box 7.3 a Mercy Inchicore Scholar describes the effect TA21–CFES has had on her life, in particular through this trusted relationship with Michelle.

Students who establish trusted networks of parents, teachers and other mentors are more likely to aspire to college degrees than students who do not. Focus group data highlight this point: Scholars who relate to their mentors, especially mentors from the same school or community, benefit most from the experience; they say the mentoring process is an ideal way to learn how to navigate the education system, whether learning about the application process, requesting financial aid, or understanding how to best transition to college life. By sharing personal experiences, students were

Box 7.2 *Impact of Mentoring and Relatable Role Models*

Michelle O'Kelly, CFES Liaison and Teacher at Mercy Inchicore

I was born in the early 1980s into a one-parent family in a flat complex in Dublin 8 (a community in Dublin that is considered low income because it has a high rate of people on social assistance and in state-provided housing). This is also an area renowned for high crime, addiction and socioeconomic disadvantage. Educational progression was not something that we thought of, as there were many other barriers to overcome before that.

School was a place where I felt that I never really fit in. I was an honors student, however I never felt like I fit into those classes, as all the girls in the class were from the nicer part of Inchicore and weren't allowed to hang around with me after school . . . I always felt a little stuck in the middle, not being able to be my real self. This feeling followed me when I progressed to third level. I was the only one from my group of friends to apply for a degree. I was also the first person in my family to progress to third level . . . I felt bad for starting to experience and enjoying new things that other members of my family couldn't and I also felt that in college I couldn't talk to people the way I would at home . . . It took three college courses and 10 years for me to square all of this off and feel completely comfortable being my true self in college and being comfortable at home to share my college experience and encourage younger family members to think about college and challenge some of their beliefs.

My personal experience has led me to believe so much in TA21–CFES. The project gives students and their families an opportunity to begin a journey in second level school which allows them to feel comfortable in their own skin and around their own family and not feel like they need to change how they speak or act to become worthy of progressing onto third level. It empowers and supports them to be comfortable with how they express themselves and not to be feeling like they have to change this in order to be accepted. It allows them to begin conversations with graduates who may not have come from a disadvantaged background and realize at a much earlier stage than I did that there are really genuine and good people in all classes of society and that they too can achieve what these people have. It also creates a small space within the family which allows everyone to become part of the conversation around education and progression, as it takes away some of the fears parents have around college because they are included in conversations about their children's future using language that is not exclusive or threatening.

Pride is a feeling that keeps coming to my mind when I think of how TA21–CFES has affected the students in Mercy Inchicore. From the individual students feeling proud of themselves through the leadership projects, to parents receiving positive feedback and leaving the school proud of their daughter, to the school community feeling proud of being part of TA21–CFES. We are all becoming proud of where we're from and are so happy to share our experiences with people.

Box 7.3 *Mentor Impact on a TA21–CFES Scholar from Mercy Secondary School, Inchicore*

I am 14 years old. I am currently in 3rd year (age 15) preparing for my Junior Certificate (first major state examination). I enjoy playing football and going out with my friends. I don't like doing homework and getting up real early in the morning for school, (but) who does?

I live in flats and have for most of my life. I live with my ma, nanny, and sister and always remember it as just us four. My da was in and out of prison for the majority of my life so I got to see very little of him. Three years ago he died. Growing up I saw the real world. My older family relations haven't really achieved much, being unemployed and on the welfare, addicted to drugs.

I want so much to get what life can offer me. I want to have a great job that I went to college and worked hard for. I want my family to be happy and have a lovely car and a big house they look forward to coming home from school to . . . I am going to be the first in my family to do my Leaving Certificate (final, school-leaving, state examination), never mind go to college.

To know I'm going to be the first to make history in my family is the best feeling in the world. TA21–CFES is really helping me during school. It makes me feel good to think that even though I come from a one-parent household there is still an opportunity for me to go to college. I also like being a part of TA21-CFES because I can relate to a lot of the teachers (mentors) including Ms. O'Kelly (Box 7.2). She makes everything so much easier for me and she knows exactly how I feel because she felt the same before. She's such an inspiration for me because she comes from the exact same background and still she achieved her dream, and she did it without the help I have today. I'm so lucky to have her along with the rest of the supporting teachers (mentors) in my school who want the best for me.

able to create networks through which they could build their knowledge of future options.

The life stories of TAP Trinity graduates from low-income backgrounds mirror those of the students they work with—precisely why they were selected as mentors. The TA21–CFES project team thought this kinship would help Scholars relate to the messages delivered by the mentors.

Even the mentors say they benefited from their participation—an unexpected bonus (Box 7.4). Mentors said they felt empowered returning to the places where they had grown up and sharing their experiences with younger students. Additionally, they found that the skills necessary for being a good mentor, such as building relationships and communicating, are useful professionally as well.

Leadership Through Service

Leadership Through Service played a critical role in the Scholars' skill development. Through implementation of community-focused service initiatives with their peers, Scholars reported feeling more autonomous, and there were notable changes in the self-efficacy and confidence among those who participated in the activities. There was variation in how the schools

Box 7.4 *Impact of Mentoring on Mentors*

Interviewer question: "What has been the positive effects of being a TA21 mentor?"

- Sarah: "Knowing that I was actually getting the point of TA21–CFES across to the girls. During one session, one of the girls told me I should be proud because I'm from Inchicore and in Trinity, and I think it hit home with her that she could be, too."

- Ava: "Chatting with the students about college experiences or aspects of college they were not aware of."

- Marian: "It's absolutely great when the mentees get engaged in a topic and ask questions that are not on the mandatory fill-in sheet."

- Andy: "Hearing the mentees be passionate about the goals they have for the future."

- Ciaran: "The concept is brilliant. The time that I did get to meet the mentees, they were all very excited to be involved. What I found most satisfying is that the students are interested in what I have to say and they valued my advice."

- John: "Seeing the students becoming more motivated and behaving better as the sessions went on, being able to have fun but get the work done as well, incorporating all the different personalities and methods. Getting to know the students and allowing them to have someone to associate with who has been where they are and has gone to college."

approached leadership activities; some schools ran projects involving an entire class, while others established a smaller leadership team that led all the activities. Schools that had broader student-led engagement in leadership practices saw a greater impact on all of their students. As a result, schools were encouraged to involve all Scholars.

For their part, Scholars stated that the leadership program empowered them to set goals for their future and taught them the importance of planning, teamwork, resilience and foresight, all *Essential Skills* applicable to both school and work. As one Scholar said, "It wasn't the teachers doing it, it was us." Others talked about how the program gave them the confidence to trust their own abilities. Leadership has a profound impact on students—yet another reason to include all students in programs such as these, rather than just a select group.

Through the development of supportive networks within the school and community, students tap into a pipeline from which they receive trusted information about higher education and careers. The Leadership Through Service practice, along with Mentoring and Pathways, builds a college going culture. Table 7.6 shows that there was a 27 percent increase in students who stated that their school was good or excellent in creating a college going environment. There was no change in the low- or high-control groups.

Table 7.6 TA21–CFES Scholar, High and Low Control Groups, Percent who Rated their School as either "Good" or "Excellent"*

	TA21-CFES Scholar		High Control		Low Control	
	Before Year One %	After Year One %	Before Year One %	After Year One %	Before Year One %	After Year One %
Creating a college-ready environment	40	67	42	32	47	44
Providing information of college entry requirements	46	66	43	33	47	43
Providing college knowledge	43	69	37	28	44	40
Providing information of financial supports for college	34	43	23	18	32	29
Providing information on how to succeed in college	44	66	43	34	51	45

* CFES U.S. does not ask this question of Scholars so no comparison is available.

Leadership Through Service also has the effect of improving not just oneself but one's community, as the same networks that encourage students to think about their future inspire them to think of others. One school, for example, created a Japanese garden within the school grounds as a reflective space for students. Another held a mental health awareness day and established a buddy system for new students within the school.

Case Studies

Creating equal access to higher education is a global challenge, the solutions to which are informed by experiences shared by different countries and spread by the thoughtful adaptation of effective models. After just one year, the TA21–CFES project demonstrated that CFES's U.S. model is adaptable to an international audience. Low-income students are actively engaging in the core practices, their aspirations for college and careers are being positively impacted, and project schools are developing a can-do culture that is transcending school boundaries.

The following case studies from Ireland—School 1 and School 2 to protect their privacy—highlight some of the early-stage lessons from implementing TA21–CFES and identify some of the necessary steps to adapt it within different national contexts.

TA21–CFES School Case Study School 1

More than 700 students are enrolled in School 1, founded by the Sisters of Mercy in 1968. The school has a large low-income population and it has also, in recent years, established active links with a higher education access program.

When the principal at School 1 decided to collaborate with Trinity College Dublin as Ireland's pilot CFES School in 2013, she ensured that staff and students could take time within the school day to plan for changes in the school's daily routine, such as the need to bring in substitutes to cover the classes of teachers on the CFES team who were involved in planning. The principal also charged each department with incorporating the three core CFES practices into its subject area.

The principal appointed an in-house team to implement the program. Every teacher in the CFES program, and every administrator in a position of leadership (e.g. deputy and/or assistant principals) was responsible for contributing in some way to the CFES School of Distinction application process.[9]

A whole-school approach: Every student in School 1 became involved with CFES. This whole-school approach, which turned every student into a TA21–CFES Scholar, encouraged a greater cultural shift across the staff and student body. It also echoed other embedded inclusive practices within the school.

Accountability: Like most initiatives, the program didn't enjoy unanimous support. Some teachers said CFES's college-or-bust message undermined the validity of other jobs and career routes, and that the strong emphasis on college might damage students who did not have the ability for higher education. Other teachers did not wish to contribute to any more out-of-classroom activities. But school leadership made it clear: Each teacher was expected to get on board and address CFES core practices in their subjects. By making it part of the planning process, the principal held individual subject departments and teachers accountable. Even teachers who were not participating in the project would be present for planning and aware of the activities. This inclusive communication about the project meant that all departments within the school were spreading the same message—that college was the goal—and it also meant that students and parents expected all staff to be on board.

Core practices: Before launching the project, the TA21–CFES team inventoried what it was already doing and examined which of its practices already fit CFES core practices. For example, School 1 already employed a peer-to-peer mentoring system that aligned with the CFES mentoring practice. In other areas, the planning process left enough time to build out areas that were lacking. In year two, the school was selected as one of the 11 TA21–CFES project schools, which were following the more specified, second-year cohort approach. This was added to their existing CFES project and they expanded their team to undertake the additional work.

School 1 implemented the core practices in several ways. Service projects included building a garden space within the school grounds, while the pathways to college and career activities included a STEM-career evening. Mentoring was kept 'in house' with a focus on peer mentoring, so that each year's group either acted as a mentor or a mentee.

Branding: The principal put the College For Every Student name at the front and center of School 1's branding, so it quickly became known as a "CFES school" in the local community—a moniker that indicated it was gaining international recognition. In the process, the CFES name supplanted the school's association with DEIS (Delivering Equality of Opportunity In Schools). By rebranding from that old state-sponsored system, synonymous with disadvantage and limited opportunities, School 1 indicated it is an ambitious, dynamic school committed to building its reputation as a beacon of excellence. A media outreach campaign in which the local newspaper was invited to all CFES events and national media was alerted about awards ceremonies and School of Distinction events, helped the school create a more positive impression in the local community.

Branding, though, is only as effective as the truth it reflects. And after working with CFES for just two years, School 1's students are already aiming higher. The number of Scholars who discuss college options with their parents and teachers increased by 60 percent after year one, and 85 percent of School 1 students went on to further or higher education. (In 2006, just 15 percent of School 1 students had gone on to further or higher education.)

Not all of the increases are necessarily attributable to CFES. School 1 had already formed some important external links before becoming part of CFES, including a formal link for educational outreach with TAP, and was on an upward trajectory when it volunteered to be the Irish pilot for CFES. In any case, the gains have led to a significant boost in school enrollment, and prospective students now face a long waiting list for entry.

Lessons from School 1: For all the research and planning behind the CFES rollout at School 1, the most important ingredient in its success has been the support of School 1's leadership and management. The principal has been unwaveringly positive—an attitude that ripples out to the staff, students, and the wider school community as they unite behind a goal of inspiring students to pursue greater things. By integrating CFES into all subject areas, departments, key posts, and sponsoring a concerted media and branding campaign, the project and its objectives have taken root at the very heart of the school's ethos. By providing time for adequate planning and reflection, School 1 cultivated continuous learning and a burgeoning college-going culture.

TA21–CFES School Case Study School 2

School 2 is a small, second-level girls' school in Dublin city, with an enrollment of 184 students. It is located in an area with high unemployment, state-supported housing, and low educational attainment. Some students, coming from families with long legacies of welfare dependence, cannot see any rewards in leaving the area—an attitude that makes it a challenge to break the cycle. Even among students eager to go to college, their families may be resistant for financial or cultural reasons. As a result, the transition can be very difficult. All staff members in the school community work with the students and their families in an attempt to support a successful transition from second level to third level.

The school began implementing TA21–CFES in 2014. It was considered a vehicle by which to make guidance and post-secondary progression a whole-school concern rather than just a matter for the guidance department. CFES's language and culture helped the school start conversations with students around their identity, how they considered they might fit into a college community, and also to address and overcome some poverty-related barriers.

CFES planning and resources: The guidance counselor presented the TA21–CFES project to all staff and discussed the practices already in place within the school that would support program development. The opportunity to share information with all staff signaled the principal's commitment that this initiative was important to the future of the school. Six teachers volunteered to join the TA21–CFES school team, with two teachers taking responsibility for each of the CFES three core practices. The TA21–CFES team agreed to meet every 2–3 weeks, with specific core practice meetings taking place more frequently at high activity points.

Branding: To make students consider the CFES experience special, the TA21–CFES team tried to create a buzz around being a Scholar and encourage students to commit to CFES activities outside of the classroom. The year started with a celebration ceremony at which all Scholars signed a memorandum of agreement to commit to the CFES practices; in return, students received a CFES Scholar pin to wear on their uniforms.

Mentoring: Each student was paired with a mentor who was a graduate of the school and/or undergraduate at Trinity College Dublin. Many mentors came from the linked access program at Trinity College Dublin. A form was sent to all mentors with a schedule of times and dates when students were available so they could choose the most suitable time. This system created a space for the mentor–mentee relationship to develop. Some sessions resulted in students missing class; some teachers were anxious about this. The mentoring sessions were structured: the Scholars had information sheets to complete before each session with their mentors.

Pathways to College and Career. Scholars visited two higher education campuses and completed assignments related to college-focused careers.

Leadership Through Service: The TA21–CFES team and Scholars were trained in leadership development at Trinity College Dublin. It took almost a whole year for students to completely embrace this practice, but when they did, it yielded results beyond all expectations in terms of Scholars' confidence, independent thinking, and resilience. Faculty resistance at the start was about students being able to manage their time and stay focused in an environment where they were the leaders. Prior to this year most of the group work was teacher-led and very prescriptive, a necessity because students were often too unruly to work on their own. When students were asked to lead a project and decide what to do on their own, it proved difficult for them. However, with persistence, the results were outstanding. The Scholars led a project to redesign an unused schoolroom into a learning space, which culminated in a launch event at which they presented the room to the wider community. The students secured industry sponsorship for the room, an exercise that expanded their network and educated them about possibilities beyond their community.

Whole-school effect of CFES: Every staff meeting included time to discuss CFES, and the principal gave the project the time and resources identified as necessary by the TA21–CFES team. Again, not all staff were convinced of the merits of the CFES concept. Some feared the program would give students false hope, if they aspired beyond their capabilities. Others felt that they did not have time, and some teachers were just set in their ways.

Within months, the CFES program won converts. Some staff who did not sign up for the team at the beginning of the year became involved in the program later as they saw the difference it was making to the school community. Originally, one lead teacher was in charge of all CFES; by the end of the year, four committed teachers helped develop the project. There is a commitment to an expanded TA21–CFES team, which will enable the program to reach scale throughout Ireland.

While the in-school planning time was valuable, the opportunity to meet with other TA21–CFES schools was an even greater boon to School 2 in terms of idea exchange, motivation, and inspiration. For example, the 11 CFES schools met three times a year. Students were apprised of the progress other institutions were making—important not just to inspire them to keep pushing forward, but also to know that they weren't alone as they participated in this new process. Educators shared ideas about leadership projects which was reported back to the students; this resulted in a healthy competition among students in terms of the impact they were having within their schools. It was important for schools to know that other schools were attempting to make these big changes. The TA21–CFES schools developed and practiced their leadership skills both nationally and internationally through participation in the CFES Conference in Burlington, VT.

Lessons from School 2: Initial resistance to the TA21–CFES project—among both students and teachers—diminished as each group became aware of the dividends of participation. Students began to sense the opportunities before them when they took ownership of space in the school as part of the Leadership Through Service project; teachers came aboard when they felt that change.

While the TA21–CFES project encourages all students to aim for college, not all students are academically capable of achieving this goal. While Pathways activities are aimed at increasing the motivation of students to work in their subjects, some were actually discouraged from participating once it became obvious that the points they needed to move on to college were out of reach. In order to keep all students in the fold, educators should be sure to inform students about possibilities for further education that do not involve college, and alternate routes to certain careers.

Conclusion

The first year of the TA21–CFES project in Ireland yielded six main lessons.

Lesson 1: Contextual adaptation of materials. All CFES materials used in the United States were reviewed and adapted to suit the Irish educational system. For instance, the financial aid process is very different in Ireland than the U.S., and the materials about aid required substantial revision.

Depending on the priority issues in each country, a customized and/or extended range of interventions may be necessary.

Another local adaptation related to the approach to mentoring. The project mainly recruited mentors from outside the school communities. This differed from the U.S. in that we insisted that students had some exposure to a college-going mentor. What worked particularly effectively was the recruitment of mentors who had entered Trinity College Dublin through the access programs for low-income students. In the future, the project intends to support all schools in building a school alumni and business mentor database.

The TA21–CFES project plans to incorporate a fourth core practice in Ireland: 21st-Century Skills. This practice will draw on the work of Bridge21,[10] which has developed a team-based, technology-mediated pedagogical approach. Teachers and students will be provided with a range of resources to support the development of a more active learning environment.

Lesson 2: The school must speak with one voice. CFES is effective only when it is supported from the top down, from senior management through the student body. In Ireland, TA21–CFES has been least effective at institutions where teachers say the program is not a priority, or where the teacher team is small, making it difficult to implement the core practices and change the attitude toward higher education. Some schools struggled under the weight of initiative overload, in which the school was involved in so many activities there was little space to support the CFES program.

Lesson 3: Develop an inclusive, personalized program. The Irish version of CFES included all the 2nd-year students in 11 schools. While U.S. schools typically engage 100 Scholars each, the Irish schools wanted to provide every student with an opportunity to explore their potential through the core practices. Perversely, this approach actually harmed some students. In some cases, students simply did not have the educational skills to meet the entry requirements for the college courses they investigated—and, recognizing the gap in their own potential, wound up even more discouraged. Students from low-income backgrounds with learning difficulties and disabilities—often not diagnosed—were doubly disadvantaged, and the project did not fully address their needs. In the future, mentors with a disability will be recruited, while pathways activities and materials will be adapted to be fully inclusive.

Lesson 4: Integrate CFES in all subject areas. In some schools, Scholars missed classes in order to participate in core practice activities. Integrating the practices into all subject areas is a more sustainable practice—though one that requires all teachers to make an explicit commitment to the project. In schools where this approach was taken, the TA21–CFES project has already had a bigger cultural impact than in schools where staff were not required to contribute. In order to get this buy-in from staff, teachers need to see the benefits it can have on classroom behavior and attendance rates. In the Irish context, emphasizing the short- and long-term benefits to students galvanized the participation of teachers.

Lesson 5: Involve families as partners. Scholars can't go it alone—they need support from their communities. While it is critical that schools build a network of organizations and businesses for students to tap into as they explore their potential, family support is just as important. Many families lack knowledge of higher education, have had bad educational experiences, or are simply busy with other commitments, so it can be difficult for them to assist Scholars as they plan their educational trajectories. That is why it is imperative to include them in the process. The schools showing the greatest positive change are those that have a) organized celebratory events that include Scholars' parents/guardians and/or b) have an open ethos, involving families, community organizations, alumni, higher education institutions, and businesses as partners working towards the same objectives. These schools have openly named their challenges, and they are showing leadership in developing and testing innovative strategies to address them. Even in the short term, this has had a notable impact on students and teachers.

Lesson 6: Tell the stories and build support. In just one year, the TA21–CFES project has amassed an impressive string of victories. It has engaged leading educators and policy makers who are invested in the project. It has identified key champions who will help secure further financial support. Schools and institutions of higher education have expressed interest in building a similar model elsewhere in Ireland. The project has also used the 'CFES School of Distinction' concept as a way to incentivize Irish schools to build the CFES project in their schools and to compete in a new national level. The school principals and liaisons are all vocal CFES champions, spreading the word on its impact across the Irish educational community. The project has been developed alongside the new "Postgraduate Certificate in 21C Teaching & Learning," which includes content on leadership, research, and inclusive education. This provides teachers with an academic scaffold for effecting change in their school communities and offers them opportunities for further professional development. It helps that Ireland is a small country, which means bringing ideas that work to scale is more realizable. Given the progress made to date, it looks promising that the project will be implemented across most areas of the country by the time the three-year funding cycle has been completed.

8 | Creating New Futures

If you share one message with your constituents from the *Guide to College & Career Readiness*, let it be this: A college education is no longer a luxury—it is a necessity. While higher education can be a ticket out of poverty, it has many other advantages beyond economic gain—including the fact that college graduates are healthier and even live longer than those without degrees.

At College For Every Student, we realize that there is a massive need to move young people, especially those from low-income backgrounds, to college and career. That's why we are committed to help one million impoverished youth across the globe attain college degrees over the next decade. Only a fraction (150,000 or so) of these students will participate directly in the CFES program. The rest will be served indirectly by practitioners—educators, community and business leaders and many others—who will adapt CFES methods to serve young people in their own schools and communities. We hope that you will take the CFES model and adapt it to support your students on the pathway to college and career readiness.

Learning from Experience and Evidence

The barriers to college are no longer defined by the differences in the courses high school students complete, since virtually all high schools now must prepare students for college. Despite this curricular parity, though, the gaps in degree attainment have grown between students born into poverty and their wealthier peers. CFES has developed a cohesive set of practices that schools, communities, businesses, and colleges can use to reverse this growing inequality. The practices are adaptable to school and community contexts. CFES has used an evidence-based approach to identify challenges, develop and test core practices, and build school–college–community networks that provide socio-cultural support that expands the horizons of low-income students living in urban and rural communities.

Understanding the Challenges

The higher education system itself, both in the United States and abroad, faces many thorny issues. Some are mere challenges; others are disturbing trends.

College costs and debt: The spiraling cost of a college education in the United States is a troubling development. In the last three decades, the price tag on a degree has soared 539 percent—more than a sixfold increase—while student loan debt now totals $1.2 trillion.[1] These runaway costs affect all students who aspire to a college education, but disproportionately affect the poor. For high-income families, college costs simply become more burdensome; for low- and even middle-income families, though, the added financial burden can make the daunting proposition of attaining a college degree even less likely.

This is a contributing factor for far too many low-income youth who opt out of college in an era when they need it the most. The widening gap in degree attainment between low-income students and their higher income peers correlates more with increasing college costs and a system that's broken than academic ability. High-income students enroll in post-secondary education at greater rates than low-income students, even when the low-income students are more academically qualified.[2]

STEM pathways: The education gap is inextricably intertwined with the economic opportunity gap: Students who go to college are the ones who get jobs in critical 21st-century fields like science, technology, engineering, and math (STEM) in the United States and other nations.

As we have seen, the STEM job and career pipeline is broken for low-income youth (Chapters 2 and 4). Employers in almost all STEM fields require their hires to have college credentials; the training represented by a degree is essential to being able to do the work. We cannot change this. What we can do, however, is enable low-income youth to pursue STEM study and careers. They have the capability. We must show them the way. Chapter 4 is filled with examples of high-impact strategies to do just that.

Our increased emphasis on job readiness (Chapters 2 and 4) has evolved over the last few years. Increasingly, we've seen the need to help our CFES Scholars become ready for the 21st-century workforce. Recently, one of our CFES Scholars, Maria, couldn't find a job after completing her bachelor's degree in psychology. She was forced to move back with her single mother and was living on food stamps. This was a wake-up call for us at CFES—a loud statement that we must ensure that our Scholars know where the 21st-century jobs are and where they will be in the next decade. Students need to understand the correlation between what they study in college and future job opportunities. We need to expose high school students to young professionals and help our students secure internships, job shadowing and other short practical experiences so that they learn about career possibilities and what they need to do to land work in the field of their choice.

Overcoming Barriers

Getting a job is an important step on a long ladder. The ladder begins as early as middle school for some young people, when we need to prepare them for college success by helping them choose a high school (especially in urban communities), build the *Essential Skills*, and develop college knowledge. By high school, students need to develop a personal, flexible plan for college and career. As part of the plan, students need to know the answers to the type of key questions about college and career listed in Chapter 2.

Paying for college: One especially important question is "How will I pay for college?" To find this answer, students should begin acquiring information in middle school or even earlier about scholarships, financial aid, and loans through exposure to older peers from similar backgrounds currently enrolled in college and/or those who have entered the workforce. Financial aid and college admissions counselors are also authentic and vital sources for this information.

Many students will wrestle with whether to take on loans to pay for college. We must recognize that not all student debt is inherently bad. It is true that some students take on larger loans than they can comfortably repay based on the earning potential of the careers they select, or find their career choices constrained by how much they are likely to earn. That, of course, can be problematic. Beyond any doubt, the worst college loan is one that does not lead to a degree. Students who take on debt and fail to graduate are still on the hook to pay back those loans—which is why CFES is so committed to giving students the skills to finish college, not just start it.

College choice: Our goal should be to enable students to graduate and earn a degree, not merely enroll in college. It is important for students to understand the ramifications of their college choice. Many well-prepared and bright students choose less selective colleges because of apparent cost, lack of guidance, or proximity to home. This phenomenon, known as undermatching, is a concern because qualified students who make this choice can end up with fewer support resources and services, decreasing their chances of degree attainment and of developing valuable networks that might later help with careers. While cost is often a factor in choosing a college, the best bargain isn't always what appears to be the least expensive at first glance. Some colleges with high sticker prices can be the best economic deal if a candidate has strong credentials and high financial need.

Navigate college pathways: It is critical that we give students every tool possible to stay in college once they get there. Academic preparation is, of course, vitally important. But we must also teach our students to be informed consumers, and to understand the limitations and opportunities inherent to the institutions they consider. In guiding young people to college and career readiness, practitioners must inform their students that certain types of colleges (as well as individual colleges and universities) have vastly different graduation rates. As a result, some higher education options present greater risks for students, so caveat emptor: Practitioners need to be aware of these pitfalls in guiding their students.

Degree attainment rates at two-year and for-profit colleges, for example, are much lower than those at most four-year public and private colleges (Chapter 2). There are multiple reasons for this. Some students drawn to two-year and for-profit institutions suffer from risk factors such as weaker academic preparation or skills and limited family support.

Cost is almost always a significant factor in the college-choice equation. Students can often get the best aid offers from colleges when they apply early, because many colleges use grants and scholarships to compete for the students they want. Aid packages can, however, be deceptive: The costs of college are not always visible. Students must remain flexible and realize there are multiple potential pathways from where they start college to where they attain their degree.

Chapter 2 offers examples of practical strategies that can support students as they complete their degrees. Persistence is complex and layered, but we know unequivocally the importance of having mentors and support networks, which practitioners can help build.

Social transformation: CFES techniques, based on the social transformation theory of change (Chapter 3), are field-proven. Recently, a team of external evaluators surveyed CFES middle school Scholars and a control group of students from similar socio-economic backgrounds. The CFES students demonstrated higher aspirations, a greater understanding of college pathways, and significantly more college readiness than their non-CFES-involved peers.

The three core practices —Mentoring, Leadership Through Service, and Pathways—can help young people develop the *Essential Skills* and build college and career knowledge. This book encourages practitioners to use the core practices and what CFES has learned over the last quarter century to help low-income students become college and career ready. These practices can be adapted to fit different cultures, resources, and settings.

One of the strengths of the CFES program is that it applies to students in all economic strata, not just those from low-income backgrounds. There are some marked differences between rural and urban schools that CFES has observed over the last quarter century. Families in urban school districts, for example, must grapple with more school-choice options than their rural counterparts. And while economists, politicians and other leaders pitched these programs as a market-driven tactic for school reform, choice has had the perverse effect of shutting some of the most vulnerable young people out of the system because their families lack sophistication and knowledge about the school marketplace. This is yet another place where mentors, educators, and practitioners can fill a vital role by helping students and their families understand the educational options available to them.

There are fewer school-choice possibilities in rural communities, but rural schools face their own challenges, including fewer options for partnerships that can produce internships, college student mentors, and exposure to young role models. Chapter 6 shares practical strategies for rural students and educators to move past these issues, although many of these tactics transcend place and apply to urban settings and even schools and communities outside the United States.

Global strategies: A pilot program in 11 Irish schools (Chapter 7) provides further evidence about not only the impact of CFES but also its adaptability. The CFES Irish project, after only two years, has had a clear impact on both students' and teachers' visions for themselves and for each other. Research data show that students have higher educational aspirations and are demonstrating greater awareness of their own potential. There is also a clear change in classroom relationships, with students seeing their teachers as more accessible and supportive. Irish educators are recognizing the positive impact of whole-school support because of the CFES model.

Get Started Now

The CFES model is built upon three core practices—Mentoring, Leadership Through Service and Pathways. These pillars help young people develop the *Essential Skills* and build college and career knowledge. To incorporate the practices into your own strategy, the book offers these lessons, among others, to educators and other practitioners who guide students toward college and career readiness:

1. *Keep it simple.* If middle school students, for example, cannot appreciate the value of a college and career readiness strategy and articulate what is happening, it is too complicated. Mentoring sessions, college knowledge lessons, and leadership development are concepts and activities students can understand. Too many education strategies have failed because students, their families, and educators cannot see the connection between the investment of time and student outcomes. Unlike many other tactics, CFES is not a trend; the value of CFES practices is timeless.

2. *Include young people as part of the solution.* The One Hundred Percent campaign at Wadleigh Secondary School in Harlem (Chapter 3), in which every member of the senior class applied to college, was built by students. In Florida, Booker High's CFES program is led by students who meet regularly to organize activities like college visits, service projects, and the MOD (Men of Distinction) squad, an all-male student group that uses peer mentoring and community role models to raise the aspirations and performance of its members. At New York City's

Richard R. Green High School, the CFES program is implemented by student leaders who plan and facilitate activities ranging from team building to the development of college and career readiness. Leadership, mentoring, and service are interwoven into the structure of student-led teams at Richard R. Green High.

3. *Mentoring* is a win–win strategy that needs to start early and continue. While the Trinity College Dublin (Chapter 7) mentors may not have started working with CFES expecting to reap personal gain, they reported feeling empowered by the experience. Develop a mentoring program that fits available resources and works for students, whether the mentors are college students, community members, corporate leaders, or peers. Many successful mentoring programs engage multiple models.

4. *Partnerships with colleges, businesses, community organizations, and even other schools are vital.* They offer valuable in-kind resources and networks. Chapter 5 shares examples of exemplary partnerships and provides tips for building and maintaining high-impact collaborations, all of which need care and feeding.

5. *Include the whole school.* The more participants and the better the buy-in, the greater the impact. Several CFES schools include all of their students in the program, and many incorporate CFES into actual classes. For example, Irish School 1 integrated CFES into all academic subjects, departments, and key positions. Developing continuous learning and a college-going culture takes time. Through substantial change and a CFES branding campaign, public perception of the institution changed, and the school became known for excellence.

6. *Successful programs have champions.* Often, these supporters are top administrators, such as Jerry Garfin, the Bronx high school principal who developed and led a partnership between his school and the University of Vermont (Chapter 5). Or Patricia Hayden, the Irish School 1 principal in Chapter 7, who had an unwaveringly positive attitude that rippled out to the staff, students and the wider school community. Hayden's can-do attitude united the school with one goal: inspire students to pursue greater things. However, not all champions occupy lofty perches (Box 8.1).

7. *Do not reinvent the wheel.* Inventory existing programs and activities and adapt them to fit CFES. As part of the planning phase, Irish educators

Box 8.1 *Ms. Robs the Dream Maker*

Consider Delores Roberts, retired family coordinator at Wadleigh Secondary School in Harlem. Known as Ms. Robs by her students, "she is tough, principled, unconventional and hands-on. She gets things done," according to Karen Judge, long-time CFES program director at Wadleigh.

"Despite obstacles, like five different principals in a decade, Delores has persevered," Judge says. "Delores personifies consistency."

This persistence and consistency have paid dividends for Wadleigh students. Since Shameka (Chapter 3) graduated from Wadleigh in 2006 and later Cornell Medical School, more than 200 others have completed associate, bachelor's, and master's degrees.

Roberts credits dozens of her CFES Scholar-Leaders, students who have stepped up to coordinate and implement a wide variety of in-school and community-based programs and projects over the years.

"Each year we adopt a theme that serves as an inspirational and motivational symbol to help students develop a "college state-of-mind," she says. "In 2006 our theme was *Believing in Achieving;* in 2008, it was *Better and Beyond;* in 2012, it was *Rock to the Challenge.*"

Roberts is proud of her students who have "beaten the neighborhood odds."

She recounts the story of Erica who, as an 11th grader, was placed at Wadleigh to serve a 90-day suspension. A bright young woman who had problems at her home school, Erica quietly listened in on meetings of the Wadleigh CFES Scholar-Leaders as they planned projects and developed programs.

"One morning Erica asked me to help her transfer to Wadleigh permanently so she could join the CFES Program," Roberts recalls. "Erica told me, 'I want to go to college. I want a fresh start.'"

Erica enrolled at Wadleigh and became a leader. Armed with a high school diploma, she went on to graduate from Lehman College.

examined their existing practices and aligned them with the CFES core practices. For example, one school already had a peer-to-peer mentoring system called "Big Brother/Sister" which fitted nicely within the mentoring practice.

8. *Include families throughout.* Incorporate families into your efforts—not just parents but also aunts and uncles, siblings, grandparents, and foster parents. When students visit colleges, invite family members, especially younger siblings, to come along. Sessions on paying for college and admissions are obvious places to include parents and guardians. If you wait to hold these sessions until grade 12, or even grade 11, it can be too late: Families need time to plan and adjust to the notion of sending their child to college. Enlist parents of young people now in college to deliver the message of how they overcame obstacles and make sure the setting, content, and language spoken reflect the culture of and are comfortable for your families.

These eight points are not the only lessons worth exporting. There are many others shared throughout the book: Be innovative. Start early. Make sure your activities and program fit the needs of your students, your school and your community.

Make a list of ideas that strike you as particularly suitable to your own situation. CFES is an adaptive model, and what is most important is that what you take away fits your needs, resources, and culture.

Create New Futures

Despite the best efforts of countless people—teachers, parents, school administrators, community leaders, public servants, and so many more—the sad truth is that the number of underserved students is growing. The needs of those students have guided the creation of this book. Our work is fueled by a passion for social justice, and we've let that passion guide every step of our careers for more than 30 years.

As important as our passion has been to our work, we recognize that data, theory, and real-world experiences are behind the incremental, pragmatic gains that support the lasting change we seek. Both of us realized early on that enthusiasm only goes so far. Results drive the day—and we approach what we do from two different, but complementary, vantage points that help us refine our models as we go along. St. John represents the world of research, Dalton the world of practice. These perspectives have allowed us to meld theory and evidence with stories and practical steps and incorporate the knowledge we have developed from working together.

But you don't need decades of practice or an advanced degree to make a difference. Caring about students, their families, and their futures can inform action when people work together. Learn from us, though, when we say that the most enduring gains you make come from decidedly non-glamorous work. Build partnerships, develop community-based networks, and reflect on evidence—what students and parents say, not just test results and data—to build pathways for better futures.

Above all, your commitment to children can be inflexible, but your approach to the work of preparing students for future success can't be. Technology is ever-changing, as are educational systems across districts, states and nations, colleges, and labor markets. The best programs accommodate for that change. Seek feedback. Reach out to people inside and outside your circle to test and make sure your work is having the desired impact. Shift strategy when it's called for and put your ego aside; we gain strength when people work together in the best interests of their students and their communities.

And, lastly, celebrate success. You're doing powerful and important work that deserves to be recognized. Share the fruits of your dream with others—there's no telling who will be inspired next.

Notes

Chapter 1

1. Dalton (2014).
2. Nellum & Hartle (2015).
3. Reardon (2012).
4. Dalton (2015).
5. Holmes et al. (1986).
6. Holmes et al. (1986)
7. Dalton (2015).
8. Holmes et al.(1986).
9. The CFES School of Distinction award, typically attained by only 15 percent of CFES Schools, recognizes that students schoolwide have benefited from the CFES program and core practices of Mentoring, Leadership Through Service, and Pathways to College.
10. U.S. Commission on Excellence in Education (1983).
11. This history is discussed by St. John (1994).
12. Trow (1974).
13. Coodley & Schmidt (2007).
14. See, for example, Finnan et al. (1995).
15. See, for example, St. John, Loescher, & Bardzell (2003).
16. See, for example, Trent & St. John (2008).
17. See, for example, St. John, Hu, & Fisher (2011).

18. St. John & Musoba (2010).

19. See St. John, Lijana, & Musoba (in press).

20. St. John (2013).

21. St. John et al. (2015).

Chapter 2

1. GE Foundation (2015).

2. Oakes (2005).

3. Dalton & Hannon (2014a).

4. St. John et al. (2015).

5. Carnevale, Smith, & Strohl (2009).

6. Quoted in presentation, the statistic is from Davidson (2011).

7. The ratios are reported by College Board based on estimates of lifetime earnings from the Bureau of Labor Statistics (BLS) 2008 earnings data (http://trend.collegboard.org/education-pays/figures-tables/lifetime-earning-education-level). There are many other reports on earning available, most of which are derived from BLS statistics.

8. GE Foundation (2015).

9. Denis St. John, Ed's son, is an artist working with Shultz Creative Group in Santa Rosa, California. He uses his computer skills in reformatting the daily "Peanuts" comics. At the same time, he is in a minority of artists in the group who still works regularly with the nibs (or pin tips) originally used by Charles Schultz for his artwork, a technique abandoned by many comic-book artists in favor of newer technologies.

10. For more background on this typology of majors and how it helps build understanding of the restructuring the K-12 educational system, see St. John (2009) and St. John et al. (2015).

11. McDermott (August 13, 2013).

12. Wikipedia (2015).

13. For example, St. John worked on projects at the University of Michigan that sought to reduce these embedded barriers for low-income students (e.g., St. John et al., 2013).

14. See for example, Adelman (1999, 2004, 2005), Berkner & Chavez (1997), Choy (2002a, 2002b), and Pelavin & Kane (1988). For an analysis of the ways these reports were used to build policy rationales, see St. John et al. (2015).

15. St. John, Daun-Barnett, & Moronski-Chapman (2013).

16. Nellum & Hartle (2015).

17. Statistics on representation and completion were generated from Census and NCES data by St. John, Daun-Barnett, & Moronski-Chapman, 2013.

18. Lynch, & Engle (2009).

19. St. John (2003, 2006); St. John et al. (2013); St. John & Noell (1989).

20. For example, Elizabeth Warren (2014) has raised public awareness that the federal government charges higher interest on student loans than it charges banks.

21. U.S. Department of Education (1983). For analyses on how this report has shaped policy, see Daun-Barnett (2008) and St. John et al. (2013).

22. Ibid.

23. Organization for Economic Cooperation and Development's "Education at a Glance" report, 2014.

24. GE Foundation (2015).

25. NBC News (2015).

26. Thelin (2004) and Goodchild (1997).

Chapter 3

1. St. John, Hu, & Fisher (2011) developed the theory of ACF using mixed methods studies. See Winkle-Wagner, Bowman and St. John (2012) for an edited volume of research papers on ACF.

2. St. John, Hu, & Fisher (2011).

3. See Winkle-Wagner, Bowman and St. John (2012) for an edited volume of research papers on ACF.

4. Winkler & Sriram (2015).

5. Becker (1964).

6. This program is used as an indicator of poverty level, as eligibility is tied to Federal Poverty Guidelines used by schools, institutions, and facilities.

7. St. John (2015).

8. Fitzgerald (2004), Lee (2004), and St. John (2002) reexamined NCES reports and longitudinal data. Daun-Barnett (2008, 2013) examined the impact of concerns about costs on educational outcomes.

9. St. John et al. (2015).

10. For an in-depth discussion of this transformation and how research on CFES students informed the refinement of ACF theory, see St. John et al. (2015).

11. For research on white flight, see Coleman (1966). His essay on social capital (Coleman, 1988) was also highly influential.

12. In these three paragraphs, we juxtapose Coleman's earlier analysis of white flight in the wake of desegregation (1966) with subsequent discussion of the core functions of social capital (Coleman, 1988). The discussion of ACF is based on findings from St. John et al. (2011) and the discussion of subsequent surveys in based on Winkler & Siram (2015).

13. Coleman (1988, p. S104).

14. Sedlacek (2004).

15. The most common method was developed by William Sedlacek (2004).

16. See, for example, McDonough (1977, 2005); Perna (2005).

17. Bourdieu (1980/1990).

18. In their study, Winkler & Sriram (2015) confirmed all three of these concepts as measurable constructs.

19. McDonough (1997).

20. St. John, Hu, & Fisher (2011).

21. St. John et al. (2015).

22. Winkler & Sriram (2015) develop related measures using their ACF student survey. More generally, for decades researchers have focused

on the role of families and parental education (e.g., Blau & Duncan, 1967; Choy, 2002a, 2002b).

23. Bourdieu (1980/1990).

24. Winkle-Wagner (2012, p. 303).

25. Pellegrino & Hilton (2012).

26. See Ravitch (2010, 2013) and St. John et al. (2015).

27. Achieve, Inc., was founded in 1996 as a bipartisan organization to raise academic standards and graduation requirements, improve assessments, and strengthen accountability in all 50 states.

Chapter 4

1. U. S. Bureau of Labor Statistics (n.d.).

2. GE Foundation (2015).

3. National Student Clearinghouse Research Center (2015).

4. Southern Education Foundation (2015).

5. Helios Education Foundation is dedicated to creating opportunities for individuals in Arizona and Florida to succeed in postsecondary education.

Chapter 5

1. United States Census defines urbanized as an area with a population of 50,000 or more people.

2. America's Promise Alliance (n.d.).

3. Ahram et al. (2011).

4. Peralta (2014).

5. St. John et al. (2015).

6. Kahlenberg & Potter (2014, p. 128)

7. St. John et al. (2015).

8. Chubb & Moe (1990).

9. Ravitch (2010).

10. Two of the four schools visited by the University of Michigan research team are small schools carved out of Christopher Columbus High School, Pelham (CIMS/Astor/GE/Pelham).

11. Dalton (1990).

Chapter 6

1. Hunkler (2008, June 3).

2. Dalton & Holmes (2005).

3. Goreham (1997).

4. Dalton (2015).

5. Dalton, Bigelow & St. John (2012).

6. Gentry (2016, p. 125).

7. Florida Department of Education (2010).

8. See Dalton, Bigelow, & St. John (2012) for the analysis of interviews that supports this claim.

Chapter 7

1. Information on the HEAR and DARE programs is available at www.accesscollege.ie.

2. Higher Education Authority (2014).

3. Higher Education Authority (2010, 2014).

4. Higher Education Authority (2014).

5. Editors' note: This adaptation of ACF took place before the completion of research leading to the addition of "concerns about careers" to ACF as discussed in Chapter 2. This is not a problem because Irish high schools have not developed thematic niches essentially requiring students to consider major preferences when choosing a high school.

6. Share (2013).

7. Hannon and O'Sullivan noted earlier in the rationale that they are not focusing on financial aid as it is not as complex a process in Ireland as it is in the U.S., but the evidence seems to point to limited understanding, at least among this age cohort, of likely costs.

8. One school used older students from within the school.

9. The award recognizes schoolwide participation in CFES and that school leadership is committed to creating and promoting a college going culture for the entire school community.

10. www.bridge21.ie

Chapter 8

1. Dalton & Hannon (2014b).
2. NCES (2014).

References

Achieve, Inc. (2012). Common Core State Standards & Career and Technical Education: Bridging the Divide Between College and Career Readiness. www.achieve.org/files/CCSS-CTE-BridgingtheDivide.pdf. Accessed June 17, 2016.

Adelman, C. (1999). Answers in the Tool Box: Academic Intensity, Attendance Patterns, and Bachelor's Degree Attainment. Washington, DC: National Center for Education Statistics.

Adelman, C. (2004). Principal Indicators of Student Academic Histories in Postsecondary Education, 1972–2000. Washington, DC: U.S. Department of Education, Institute of Education Sciences.

Adelman C. (2005). Moving into Town and Moving On: The Community College in the Lives of Traditional-age Students. Washington, DC: U.S. Department of Education.

Ahram, R., Stembridge, A., Fergus, E., & Noguera, P. (2011). Framing Urban School Challenges: The Problems to Examine when Implementing Response to Intervention. RTI Action Network. Available online at: www.rtinetwork.org/learn/diversity/urban-school-challenges. Accessed June 17, 2016.

America's Promise Alliance. (n.d.). www.gradnation.org/sites/default/files/18006_CE_BGN_Full_vFNL.pdf?_ga=1.244939654.263311406.1466182042 . Accessed June 17, 2016.

Anderson, R. E. (2008). Implications of the Information and Knowledge Society for Education. In *International Handbook of Information Technology in Primary and Secondary Education* (pp. 5–22). Springer US.

Becker, G. S. (1964). *Human Capital: A Theoretical and Empirical Analysis with Special Reference to Education.* New York: Columbia University.

Battiste, M. (2009). Naturalizing Indigenous Knowledge in Eurocentric Education. *Canadian Journal of Native Education,* 32(1): 5.

Bennis, W. G., & Nanus, B. (2004). *Leaders.* HarperBusiness Essentials.

Berkner, L., & Chavez, L. (1997). Access to Postsecondary Education for the 1992 High School Graduates. Washington, DC: U.S. Dept. of Education, Office of Educational Research and Improvement.

Blau, P. M. and Duncan, O. D. (1967). *The American Occupational Structure.* New York: Wiley.

Bourdieu, P. (1980/1990). *The Logic of Practice* (trans. R. Nice). Stanford, CA: Stanford University.

Carnevale, A. P., Smith, N., & Strohl, J. (2009) Help Wanted, Projections of Jobs and Education Requirements through 2018. In R. Romano, & H. Kasper (Eds.), *Occupational Outlook for Community College Students: New Directions for Community Colleges,* No. 146. New York: Wiley.

Choy, S. P. (2002a). Access & Persistence: Findings from 10 Years of Longitudinal Research on Students. Washington, DC: American Council on Education.

Choy, S. P. (2002b). Findings from The Condition of Education, 2002: Nontraditional undergraduates. Washington, DC: National Center for Education Statistics.

Chubb, J. E., & Moe, T. M. (1990). Politics, Markets, and America's Schools. Washington, DC: The Brookings Institution.

Coleman, J. S. (1966). Equality of Education Opportunity Study. ICPR 3689-v 3. Ann Arbor, MI: Inter-University Consortium for Political and Social Research. 2007–04–27. Available online at: https://eric.ed.gov/?id=ED012275 .

Coleman, J. S. (1988). Social Capital in the Creation of Human Capital. *American Journal of Sociology,* 94: S95-S120. doi: 10.2307/2780243

Coodley, L., & Schmitt, P. A. (2007). *Napa: The Transformation of an American Town.* Charleston, SC: Arcadia.

Dalton, R. (1990). *The Student's Guide To Good Writing: Building Writing Skills For Success in College.* New York: College Board.

Dalton, R. (2013, January 22). Creating a College Culture Nationwide: Big Vision in a Small Town. *The Addison Eagle.*

Dalton, R. (2014, December 22). A Better Way to Climb the Ladder to College Success. Retrieved December 22, 2015, from: www.huffington post.com/matthew-lynch-edd/a-better-way-to-climb-the_b_6366210. html

Dalton, R. (2015). The Skills Gap and the New Economy: Implications for Low-income Students. Fairfield, CT: GE Foundation.

Dalton, R., Bigelow, V., & St. John, E. P. (2012). College For Every Student: A Model for Postsecondary Encouragement in Rural Schools. In R. Winkle-Wagner., P. J. Bowman, & E. P. St. John (Eds.), *Expanding Postsecondary Opportunity for Underrepresented Students: Theory and Practice of Academic Capital Formation.* Readings on Equal Education (Vol. 26, pp. 181–204). New York: AMS.

Dalton, R., & Hannon, C. (2014a). A Better Way to Climb the Ladder to College Success. *The Huffington Post.* TheHuffingtonPost.com, published December 22, 2014. Web. Accessed 17 December 2015.

Dalton, R., & Hannon, C. (2014b). A Call to Action: One Million More Low–Income Students Attain College Degrees by 2025. White Paper. Available online at: www.collegefes.org/pdfs/One-Million-More-White-Paper.pdf

Dalton, R., & Holmes, D. (2005). *Peak Experiences: Raising Aspirations and Educational Achievement of Rural Youth in Adirondack Communities.* Tallahassee, FL: Foundation for Excellent Schools.

Dalton, R., & Mills, J. (2008, January). A Learning Curve: Poor Students in Rural Districts Can Achieve a College Education. *Times Union,* pp. B1–B3.

Daun-Barnett, N. (2008). Preparation and Access: A Multi-level Analysis of State Policy Influences on the Academic Antecedents to College Enrollment. Ph.D. dissertation: University of Michigan.

Daun-Barnett, N. (2013). Access to College: A Reconsideration of the National Education Longitudinal Study (NELS). *Educational Policy,* 27(1): 3–32.

Davidson, C. N. (2011). *Now You See It: How the Brain Science of Attention Will Transform the Way We Live, Work, and Learn.* New York: Viking.

Finnan, C. R., St. John, E. P., McCarthy, J., & Slovacek, S. P. (Eds.). (1995). *Accelerated Schools in Action: Lessons from the Field*. Thousand Oaks, CA: Corwin Press.

Fitzgerald, B. K. (2004). Federal Financial Aid and College Access. In E. P. St. John (Ed.), *Public Policy and College Access: Investigating the Federal and State Roles in Equalizing Postsecondary Opportunity. Readings on Equal Education* (Vol. 19, pp. 1–28). New York: AMS.

Florida Department of Education. (2010). School District and State Public Accountability Report. Retrieved March 30, 2011, from: http://doeweb-prd.doe.state.fl.us/eds/nclbspar/year0910/nclb0910.cfm?dist_schl=23_81

Gamage, D. T., & Pang, N. S. K. (2003). *Leadership and Management in Education: Developing Essential Skills and Competencies*. Chinese University Press.

GE Foundation. (2015). The Skills Gap and the New Economy: Implications for Low-income Students. White Paper. Available online at: www.collegefes.org/pdfs/Skills_Gap.pdf. Accessed June 17, 2016.

Gentry, D. (2016). Pursuing College in Rural America. In *I'm First! Guide to College*. Bethesda, MD: Center for Student Opportunity.

Goodchild, L. F. (1997). Contemporary Undergraduate Education: An Era of Alternatives and Reassessment. *Theory Into Practice*, 36(2): 123–131.

Goreham, G. (1997). *Encyclopedia of Rural America: The Land and People*. Santa Barbara, CA: ABC-CLIO.

Heckman, J. J., & Rubinstein, Y. (2001). The Importance of Noncognitive Skills: Lessons from the GED Testing Program. *American Economic Review*, 145–149.

Higher Education Authority (HEA). (2010). Mid-term Review of National Plan for Equity of Access to Higher Education. Dublin.

Higher Education Authority (HEA). (2014). Towards the Development of a New National Plan for Equity of Access to Higher Education. Dublin.

Hoff, K. S. (1999). Leaders and Managers: Essential Skills Required Within *Higher Education. Higher Education, 38*(3): 311–331.

Holmes, D., Dalton, R., Erdmann, D., Hayden, T., and Roberts, A. (1986). Frontiers of Possibility: Report of the National College Counseling Project. Burlington, VT: University of Vermont, Instructional Development Center.

Hunkler, E. (June 3, 2008). College For Every Student. *Adirondak Daily Enterprise.* Retrieved January 3, 2016 from: http://adirondackdaily enterprise.com/page/content.detail/id/500786/College-for-Every-Student.html?nav=5008

James, D. W., Jurich, S., & Estes, S. (2001). Raising Minority Academic Achievement: A Compendium of Education Programs and Practices.

Kahlenberg, R. D., & Potter, H. (2014). *A Smarter Charter: Finding What Works for Charter Schools and Public Education.* New York: Teachers College.

Lauff, E., & Ingels, S. (January 2014) Education Longitudinal Study of 2002 (ELS: 2002): A First Look at 2002 High School Sophomores 10 Years Later. National Center for Education Statistics. Available online at: http://nces.ed.gov/pubs2014/2014363.pdf

Lee, J. B. (2004). Access Revisited: A Preliminary Reanalysis of NELS. In E. P. St. John (Ed.), *Public Policy and College Access: Investigating the Federal and State Roles in Equalizing Postsecondary Opportunity, Readings on Equal Education* (Vol. 19, pp. 87–96). New York: AMS.

Lynch, M., & Engle, J. (2009). Charting a Necessary Path: The Baseline Report of the Access to Success Initiative. Washington, DC: The Education Trust & NASH (National Association of System Heads).

McDermott, C. (August 13, 2013). Researchers Explore Factors Behind Mismatched College Choices, *Chronicle of Higher Education.* Available online at: http://chronicle.com/article/Researchers-Explore-Factors/141095/. Accessed June 17, 2016.

McDonough, P. M. (1997). *Choosing Colleges: How Social Class and Schools Structure Opportunity.* Albany, NY: SUNY.

McDonough, P. M. (2005). Counseling and College Counseling in America's High Schools. *State of College Admission*, 107–121.

National Student Clearinghouse Centre. (2015). High School Benchmarks 2015: National College Progression Rates. Available online at: https://nscresearchcenter.org/hsbenchmarks2015/. Accessed June 17, 2016.

NBC News. (2015). Many College Freshmen Don't Know How Much they're Paying or Borrowing for School. Available online at: www.nbc news.com/feature/freshman-year/many-college-freshmen-dont-know-how-much-theyre-paying-or-n415521. Accessed June 17, 2016.

Nellum, C. J., & Hartle, T. W. (2015). Where Have All the Low-income Students Gone? Higher Education Today. Washington, DC: American Council on Education. Available online at: http://higheredtoday.org/2015/11/25/where-have-all-the-low-income-students-gone/

Oakes, J. (1985/2005). *Keeping Track: How Schools Structure Inequality.* New Haven, CT: Yale University.

OECD (2014), Education at a Glance 2014: OECD Indicators, OECD Publishing. http://dx.doi.org/10.1787/eag-2014-en. Accessed June 17, 2016.

Pelavin, S. H., & Kane, M. B. (1988). Minority Participation in Higher Education. Prepared for the U.S. Department of Education, Office of Planning, Budget and Evaluation. Washington, DC: Pelavin Associates.

Pellegrino, J. W., & Hilton, M. L. (Eds.). (2013). Education for Life and Work: Developing Transferable Knowledge and Skills in the 21st Century. Washington, DC: National Academies.

Peralta, K. (2014, November 27). Native Americans Left Behind in the Economic Recovery. Retrieved February 15, 2016, from: www.usnews.com/news/articles/2014/11/27/native-americans-left-behind-in-the-economic-recovery

Perna, L. W. (2005). A Gap in the Literature: The Influence of the Design, Operations, and Marketing of Student Aid Programs on the Formation of Family College-going Plans and Resulting College-going Behaviors of Potential Students. *Journal of Student Financial Aid,* 35(3), 7–15.

Ravitch, D. (2010). The Death and Life of the Great American School System: How Testing and Choices are Undermining Education. New York: Basic.

Ravitch, D. (2013). *Reign of Error: The Hoax of the Privatization Movement and the Danger to America's Public Schools.* New York: Vintage.

Reardon, S. (2012). The Widening Academic Achievement Gap Between the Rich and the Poor. *Community Investments,* 24(2): 19–39.

Reiner, A. (2013, June 19). City Teens Uncowed by Rural Visit. Retrieved June 17, 2016, from www.pressrepublican.com/news/local_news/city-teens-uncowed-by-rural-visit/article_b1bb5dd5-dad9-5416-9c0f-5add898442ee.html

Savery, J. R. (2015). Overview of Problem-based Learning: Definitions and Distinctions. *Essential Readings in Problem-Based Learning: Exploring and Extending the Legacy of Howard S. Barrows,* 5.

Sedlacek, W. E. (2004). *Beyond the Big Test: Noncognitive Assessment in Higher Education.* San Francisco: Jossey-Bass.

Share, M. (2013). Ripples of Hope: The Family and Community Impact of Trinity College Dublin access graduates. Trinity College, Dublin: Children's Research Centre.

Sinclair, S., McKendrick, J. H., & Scott, G. (2010). Failing Young People? Education and Aspirations in a Deprived Community. *Education, Citizenship and Social Justice,* 5(1), 5–20.

Southern Education Foundation. (2015). A New Majority Research Bulletin: Low-income Students Now a Majority in the Nation's Public Schools. Available online at: www.southerneducation.org/getattachment/4ac62 e27-5260-47a5-9d02-14896ec3a531/A-New-Majority-2015-Update-Low-Income-Students-Now.aspx. Accessed June 17, 2016.

St. John, E. P. (1994). Prices, Productivity and Investment: Assessing Financial Strategies in Higher Education. ASHE/ERIC Higher Education Report, No. 3. Washington, DC: George Washington University, School of Education and Human Development.

St. John, E. P. (2002). *The Access Challenge: Rethinking the Causes of the New Inequality.* Policy Issue Report No. 2002-01. Bloomington, IN: Indiana Education Policy Center.

St. John, E. P. (2003). *Refinancing the College Dream: Access, Equal Opportunity, and Justice for Taxpayers.* Baltimore, MD: Johns Hopkins University.

St. John, E. P. (2006). *Education and the Public Interest: School Reform, Public Finance, and Access to Higher Education.* Dordrecht, The Netherlands: Springer.

St. John, E. P. (2009). *College Organization and Professional Development: Integrating Moral Reasoning and Reflective Practice.* New York: Routledge.

St. John, E. P. (2013). *Research, Actionable Knowledge, and Social Change: Reclaiming Social Responsibility through Research Partnerships:* Sterling, VA: Stylus.

St. John, E. P., Bigelow, V. M., Lijana, K., & Masse, J. (2015). *Left Behind: Urban High Schools and the Failure of Market Reform.* Baltimore, MD: Johns Hopkins University Press.

St. John, E. P., Daun-Barnett, N. J., & Moronski-Chapman, K. (2013). *Public Policy and Higher Education*. New York: Routledge.

St. John, E. P., Hu, S., & Fisher, A. S. (2011). *Breaking Through the Access Barrier: How Academic Capital Formation can Improve Policy in Higher Education*. New York: Routledge.

St. John, E. P., Lijana, K., & Musoba, G. M. (in press). *Using Action Inquiry in Education Reform: Organizing Guide for Improving Pathways to College*. Sterling, VA: Stylus Press.

St. John, E. P., Loescher, S. A., & Bardzell, J. S. (2003). *Improving Reading and Literacy in Grades 1–5: A Resource Guide to Research-based Programs*. Thousand Oaks, CA: Corwin.

St. John, E. P., Massé, J. C., Fisher, A. S., Moronski-Chapman, K., & Lee, M. (2013). Beyond the Bridge: Actionable Research Informing the Development of a Comprehensive Intervention Strategy. *American Behavioral Scientist*, 0002764213515233

St. John, E. P., & Musoba, G. D. (2010). *Pathways to Academic Success: Expanding Opportunity for Underrepresented Students*. New York: Routledge.

St. John, E. P., & Noell, J. (1989). The Impact of Financial Aid on Access: An Analysis of Progress with Special Consideration of Minority Access. *Research in Higher Education*: 30(6): 563–582.

Stamford Eighth-Grader Changing Students' Lives, One Hard Drive At A Time. (2015, March 3). Retrieved June 17, 2016, from http://stamford.dailyvoice.com/schools/stamford-eighth-grader-changing-students-lives-one-hard-drive-at-a-time/522000/

Thelin, J. R. (2004). *A History of American Higher Education*. Baltimore, MD: Johns Hopkins University.

Trent, W. T., & St. John, E. P. (Eds.). (2008). *Resources, Assets, and Strengths Among Successful Diverse Students: Understanding the Contributions of the Gates Millennium Scholars Program*. Readings on Equal Education, Vol. 23. New York: AMS.

Trow, M. (1974). *Problems in the Transition from Elite to Mass Higher Education*. New York: McGraw-Hill.

United States Department of Education. National Commission on Excellence in Education. (1983). A Nation at Risk: The Imperative for

Educational Reform: A Report to the Nation and the Secretary of Education, United States Department of Education. Washington, DC: The Commission.

U.S. Bureau of Labor Statistics. (n.d.). Occupational Employment Projections to 2022: *Monthly Labor Review*. Available online at: www.bls.gov/opub/mlr/2013/article/occupational-employment-projections-to-2022.htm. Accessed June 17, 2016.

Warren, E. (2014). *A Fighting Chance*. New York: Metropolitan.

Williams, T. R. (2005). Exploring the Impact of Study Abroad on Students' Intercultural Communication Skills: Adaptability and Sensitivity. *Journal of Studies in International Education*, 9(4), 356–371.

Winkle-Wagner, R. (2012). Academic Capital Formation: Can it Help Untangle Confusion about Social Stratification in the Study of College Students? In R. Winkle-Wagner, P. J. Bowman, & E. P. St. John (Eds.), *Expanding Postsecondary Opportunity for Underrepresented Students: Theory and Practice of Academic Capital Formation* (pp. 293–306). Readings on Equal Education, Vol. 26. New York: AMS.

Winkle-Wagner, R., Bowman, P. J., & St. John, E. P. (Eds.). (2012). *Expanding Postsecondary Opportunity for Underrepresented Students: Theory and Practice of Academic Capital Formation*. Readings on Equal Education, Vol. 26. New York: AMS.

Wikipedia. (2015). "Undermatching" Wikipedia: The Free Encyclopedia. Wikimedia Foundation, date last updated (January 30, 2015). Web. Accessed September 3, 2015. Available online at: https://en.wikipedia.org/wiki/Undermatching

Winkler, C. & Sriram, R. (2015). Development of a Scale to Measure Academic Capital in High-risk College Students, *The Review of Higher Education*, 38(4): 565–587.

Index

Note: Page references to figures and tables are in *italic*.

tutoring 80, 81
Twenty-First Century Scholars,
   Indiana 13, 47, 52, 53
two-year colleges 29, 30, 35;
   degree attainment 24, *28*, 29,
   161

undermatching 27, 161
University of Vermont-Christopher
   Columbus High School
   partnership 93, 94–96
urban schools 17, 23, 87, 88–89,
   90–91, 105–106, 114, 162;
   adaptability 113–114; partner
   organizations 88, 93–98
urban students 17, 88, 90, 91–93,
   114; Leadership Through
   Service 102–103, 108, 109;

mentoring 98–100, 108;
   perseverance 107–108,
   112–113; raised aspirations
   110–111

virtual support, CFES 10, 75, 122,
   126

Wadleigh Secondary School,
   Harlem 44, 45, 46, 91, 163,
   165
Washington State Achievers 47,
   52, 53
West Point Military Academy 73,
   74
Willsboro, New York 91–93, 117,
   122, 123
Winkle-Wagner, Rachelle 54

Taylor & Francis eBooks

Helping you to choose the right eBooks for your Library

Add Routledge titles to your library's digital collection today. Taylor and Francis ebooks contains over 50,000 titles in the Humanities, Social Sciences, Behavioural Sciences, Built Environment and Law.

Choose from a range of subject packages or create your own!

Benefits for you

>> Free MARC records
>> COUNTER-compliant usage statistics
>> Flexible purchase and pricing options
>> All titles DRM-free.

Benefits for your user

>> Off-site, anytime access via Athens or referring URL
>> Print or copy pages or chapters
>> Full content search
>> Bookmark, highlight and annotate text
>> Access to thousands of pages of quality research at the click of a button.

REQUEST YOUR **FREE** INSTITUTIONAL TRIAL TODAY	**Free Trials Available** We offer free trials to qualifying academic, corporate and government customers.

eCollections – Choose from over 30 subject eCollections, including:

Archaeology	Language Learning
Architecture	Law
Asian Studies	Literature
Business & Management	Media & Communication
Classical Studies	Middle East Studies
Construction	Music
Creative & Media Arts	Philosophy
Criminology & Criminal Justice	Planning
Economics	Politics
Education	Psychology & Mental Health
Energy	Religion
Engineering	Security
English Language & Linguistics	Social Work
Environment & Sustainability	Sociology
Geography	Sport
Health Studies	Theatre & Performance
History	Tourism, Hospitality & Events

For more information, pricing enquiries or to order a free trial, please contact your local sales team: www.tandfebooks.com/page/sales

Routledge
Taylor & Francis Group

The home of
Routledge books

www.tandfebooks.com